SCOTT~~ISH FOLKLORE~~

SCOTTIS]

MW01290009

REMINISCENSES OF
ABERDEENSHIRE

First Edition 1895
Duncan Anderson

New Edition 2019
Edited by Tarl Warwick

1

SCOTTISH FOLKLORE

COPYRIGHT AND DISCLAIMER

FOREWORD

This fine book is a fairly lengthy collection of various lore related to the authors' recollection of his early life in Scotland and some of the stories and gossip of the day- a fine time and place for strange tales indeed, as the middle of the 19th century is marked by the slow advance of the industrial and urban into areas which, even in the more developed parts of the world, had been relatively pastoral and extremely folkish.

The disappearance of folklore is noted in the introduction itself; perhaps this is important because since this book was written, more than a century has elapsed- several more generations have come and gone and lost more and more of their folklore along the way- it is an odd truth that disconnectedness between kin and neighbor increases as human communication and technology incline, wiping out local lore even while those same advances attempt to frenetically stockpile, publish, and archive it; I have seen this myself- since I was a child in the 1990s the cohesion of small Vermont communities has significantly reduced, while folklore from this same area has been compiled and released a hundred times in literature alone over the same period, driven by its desirability and therefore profit motive.

As an occultist my main interest in this work deals with some of the (often quite odd) tales herein which speak of cryptids and witchery and certain now-outdated folk traditions especially related, there in Scotland, to Christendom and its folkish component at that time; we see that this particular facet- the folkishness of religion- is still quite common and evident, even in religions that shun the idea and consider it heretical such as Islam or certain pagan paths.

SCOTTISH FOLKLORE

Treatments here of folklore related to ritual behavior are also of note- especially the humorous tale of one man (a friend of the author) forced to quickly leave a feast he'd been invited to because through his apparent inebriation he had offered to marry not one but several local females, all of which apparently accepted the proposal. Tales of the local madman forcing a schoolboy to march around the town square reciting the Bible at hazard of being hit with a stick if he got it wrong are humorous, if not necessarily of great true spiritual import. Nonetheless, this work is anecdotal and deals with a very localized place and time, and is not a broad overview of Scottish folklore at large, which otherwise the title might have suggested.

As a slight tip here for the reader; to properly comprehend some of the Scottish references here, in quotation, where a thick accent and numerous non-English words are included, it makes sense to read it out loud in a Scottish accent. By sounding it out it is often possible to more or less understand what is being said.

This edition of "Scottish Folklore" has been carefully edited for format and grammar. Care has been taken to retain all original intent and meaning.

SCOTTISH FOLKLORE

INTRODUCTION

By these mysterious ties, the busy power
Of memory her ideal train preserves
Entire; or when they would elude her watch,
Reclaims their fleeting footsteps from the waste
Of dark oblivion.

Akenside.

The late Dean Ramsay of Edinburgh, in the preface
to his Reminiscences, says, "It is interesting to preserve national
peculiarities which are passing away from us." The remark is one
that strikes with peculiar force every Scotchman, and as the
years go by, and those who capped our best stories with some of
their own, join the majority, the feeling deepens with us that the
opportunities of preserving such peculiarities are indeed very
materially lessening. Not much more than a decade of years has
passed since I was invited to meet, at the house of an intimate
friend, two or three acquaintances, formerly residents of Quebec,
but whose lines had now fallen to them in other places.

We were all of us of that class, that, loving Scotland as it
should be loved, enjoyed the pleasure of telling, and hearing
told, the stories of our native land. It need scarcely be remarked
that the sma' hours were reached long before we thought of
separating. Before, however, Auld Lang Syne was sung, the
host remarked, "What a pity that these stories that have been told
here tonight should be lost! Could a stenographer have been
stationed within earshot, what an interesting paper might he have
supplied to thousands of readers, and would not the object be
thus gained of rendering imperishable what after all, may, in a

5

few years, be difficult, perhaps impossible, to recall?"

This remark struck us all, and we then agreed, that, if ever a convenient season came, we would put our heads and pens together, and endeavor to do, each in his way, what the reporter might have done for us.

That convenient season, however, never came, and when I looked around me only lately, I was painfully reminded that it could now never come. Impelled by a feeling of regret, I resolved to do alone, in a humble way, what might have been so much better done by us all. I felt like the subaltern under fire, who knows that, however unfit he may be, yet it is still his duty to lead on, when his superior officers have been laid low on the field of battle. But how to perform my duty in the best way, I was at a loss to determine. The mere stringing of anecdotes together did not take my fancy, and it would be difficult to follow in the footsteps of such men as Ramsay and O'Rell, without provoking a comparison that might be at least unpleasant, and I had, in consequence, to relinquish all idea of relating almost anything except what was mainly my own. Another way then lay open to me, for which I had, I believed, one special qualification, and that way I adopted. So far as my recollection of individuals, and of circumstances connected with them, was concerned, memory never failed me. Like the musician whom two or three notes will often enable to repeat the almost forgotten melody, so, on recalling some acquaintance of my early years, the outline, at first only dim and indistinct, becomes gradually clothed with a flood of light, and the minutest traits of appearance and character, and life and sayings, stand out boldly as if I had been contemplating them but yesterday. This decided me. I had no intention of creating characters to suit my story, if indeed story it might be called, for like Canning's needy knifegrinder, I might say "Story? God bless your honor, I have none to tell, Sir," but there were men and women that I had known nearly a half century ago, and these I would call as witnesses, and make them once more tell their own tale. In telling it, they would, at the same time, give a faithful picture of a quiet Aberdeenshire village and parish, about forty or fifty years ago.

Why I have used on my title-page, "From Pinafore to Gown," is readily enough explained. I quickly found that the materials on hand would soon swell to the proportions of a somewhat unwieldy volume, and I imagined that what I recollected of Sillerton from boyhood till I entered college, would be sufficient, in size and quality, to test my chances of success as a faithful historian of folk-lore. I have contrived to throw what must prove a very flimsy veil over places and individuals, but I feel persuaded that if any one finds himself or his friends portrayed in these humble pages, the recognition of the likeness will not, under any circumstances, be accompanied with pain.

I may add that I have attempted to sketch Sillertonians, certainly not as they should have been, but such as they were ; if I fail to interest the reader, I must pay the penalty of failure; if success crowns my efforts, I shall not, in that case, present my

P. P. C. card. D. A.

CHAPTER I

MY PINAFORE

My eyes are dim with childish tears,
My heart is idly stirred;
For the same sound is in my ears
Which in those days I heard.

Wordsworth.

Pinafore, did I say? Yes, it was a blue pinafore that I
wore. Whether it was intended for ornament or use, or perhaps
for both purposes, I cannot now well say, but yet the color and
pattern are as well stamped upon memory's page as if I had worn
the garment but yesterday. And yet sixty years, more or less,
make a long telescope through which an old man observes a
pinafore that he wore when his wavy locks hung in ringlets over
his shoulders. Sixty years, more or less, did I say? Ah! certainly,
not less, not less. I like truth under any circumstances, although
sometimes it may be a bitter pill to swallow, when swallowing is
in order.

But then, what of more? Well, I feel comparatively
young still. Let me hear the whir of a hardwood partridge among
the maple branches in the dear month of October, and then what
eye is brighter, what foot is fleeter, than mine? Let a
north shore salmon, fresh from the icy seas of Labrador, get upon
my line, and is it a feeble hand that guides him through swirl and
pool to a quiet corner, or a feeble voice that joins in the joyous
whoop that my Indian gives as he lays the glittering beauty on
the pebbly shore?

But yet the silken ringlets went long ago, when my

8

mother, with tears coursing down her cheeks, cut them all away, and selected only one to fill that locket that has hung unworn now for nearly fifty years. But there are curls yet; alas! not everywhere, but yet in fair abundance, and with a few threads of silver among them, and making them look just as if a sprinkling of snowflakes had touched them gently amid the frolics of the Christmas time. Not less then, but say more. But writing of snowflakes reminds me of the first time that any one seemed to notice that Father Time had taken liberties with me. A daughter who had spent a few years in a foreign land, and who never failed to break down when the choir of the church where she worshiped sung Payne's beautiful hymn; "Home, Sweet Home!" sent us unexpected tidings of an intended visit. The wintry morning was bitterly cold- the loud whistle of the approaching train had, a few minutes before, intimated its arrival; the old flag was run up to the mast-head; the merry jingling of sleigh-bells was heard, and our long absent one was soon folded in our arms.

There were no dry eyes there, for do they not overflow both at the touch of joy as well as of sorrow? Looking at me through her blinding tears, she said, suiting the action to the word, "Father, let me brush the snow away from your beard.", "Ah, Janie, that snow can never be brushed away. It is God's harbinger of the winter of age. It has come to stay."

To return to my pinafore. I cannot describe exactly the pattern, yet I could swear to it among a thousand. Like the 'willow' pattern on our own dinner sets, so the 'pinafore' pattern must have come down to us for many generations, and for aught that I know very probably suggested the idea to the artist who had the honor of designing the Star-spangled Banner. Why I so clearly recollect that pinafore I have an idea. There seems to be, at times, small hooks that pin things firmly to memory, and there was one in this instance. It was a beautiful Sunday morning in spring. We were all dressed accordingly. Accordingly means ready for church, the service in which commenced in those days at the very reasonable hour of noon. Father had arrived from a distance the night before, and had brought small presents for the little ones. Mine was a somewhat peculiar imitation watch, not in nickel or tin, as nowadays, but in some species of delfware that shone like old gold. With this stuck in a pocket put in my new pinafore evidently for the occasion, I strolled out to the churchyard, which lay just behind the village, my object being to gather a bouquet of gowatis, and to enjoy myself generally that is, with such decorum as the Sabbath, or at least Scottish parents, demanded of little folks in Scotland in those days. Wandering among the grassy mounds that marked the places where "The rude forefathers of the hamlet slept," and gathering my bouquet of daisies and primroses, I found myself at the low window of the cobbler's shop which looked out upon the churchyard.

I had never looked in at that window before. Out of it I had often looked, for Sandy Simms, the village shoemaker, and I, notwithstanding the disparity of ages, were good friends. Sandy loved to tell a good story, and to hear one as well, and when the hobbledehoys came to have their shoes patched, or to get irons fastened upon the toes of their heavy boots in preparation for a game of football, for which pastime the village boys of Sillerton were famous over at least a dozen parishes, Sandy's tongue and rozetty ends kept good time together. What the forte was that charmed the rustics I cannot now remember; there must, however, have been no small art displayed, seeing that the souter's shop almost rivaled the blacksmith's smithy, while we little folks, if we did not quite understand the gist of all we heard, yet never failed to show unbounded delight, by opening not only ears, but also eyes and mouth, at the souter's eloquence. Personally, then, if, indeed, an urchin of my years could lay claim to a distinct and separate personality, I owed Sandy no grudge. His tongue had never suggested to me that it was time for small boys to be jogging homewards, nor had his elison ever expedited my movements in that direction. On the other hand the genial souter had been kindness itself personified.

What then could have prompted me to do anything to hurt the feelings or property of my friend I am unable to say. That I should at that moment, in that quiet churchyard, on that calm and beautiful Sunday morning, draw out of my pocket that newly-acquired watch and with it coolly and deliberately, as if from malice prepense, break a pane of glass in the cobbler's window, has proved to be a problem as hard of solution as the squaring of the circle has been to the long-baffled mathematician. Was it the result of pride in the possession of that spurious imitation of a timekeeper; did convenience snug stir up the treacherous inclination; or was it possible that the very deil himself whispered in the ear of my heart to prove my manhood by breaking the window of the souter's workshop? I need not say how soon remorse came. I felt that day in church as if I had not merely broken a pane of glass, but as if I had murdered the souter himself. I could scarcely say my short prayer that night, and for clays after, my punishment was almost greater than I could bear. Oh! dear Tom Hood! You must, when a boy, have cracked some friendly cobbler's window unprovoked, else never could you have written these lines;

> "O Heaven ! to think of their white souls,
> And mine so black and grim!
> I could not share in childish prayer,
> Nor join in evening hymn:
> Like a Devil of the Pit I seem'd
> 'Mid holy Cherubim!"

For months after I would have walked a Scotch mile rather than pass that wretched window with the patched pane of glass in it, and I never had the courage to enter Sandy's workshop again. Alas! It is conscience that makes cowards of us

11

all. What wonder then was it that my little ears ceased to listen to the old stories that I had so often heard before from the eloquent lips of the kindly souter, or that I had never forgotten the blue pinafore that I had worn on that eventful and sadly-to-be-lamented Sunday morning?

CHAPTER II

SILLERTON AND ITS SURROUNDINGS

"How still the morning of the hallowed day;
Mute is the voice of rural labor; hushed
The plowboy's whistle and the milkmaid's song."

Grahame.

Sillerton, after all, was a strange name for a quiet, impecunious village, or rather quiet country parish. In fact the godfathers and godmothers of that ilk must have been wags in their way, and given the name on the Lucus a non hicendo principle, for siller did not lie about promiscuously in the village, or in the parish either. It is true that there were considerable operations in timber carried on in the neighborhood, but these, beyond giving a miserable wage to a few men, filled the pockets of the laird only, who knew well how to earn and how to keep his profits.

There was also a distillery that manufactured a limited quantity of the genuine mountain dew, but very limited that quantity must have been, seeing that the manager, when trying to sell his goods one market day to a jolly farmer who was noted for the quantity and quality of his liquor, and being told that unless he lowered his prices he might shut up shop altogether, at once retorted "Na, na, man; as lang's we hae the same manager and the same partners we are quite capable of drinking the haill browst oursels." It is almost needless to say that the bibulous manager got an order on the spot. Sillerton then was somewhat like Rob Rorison's bonnet. "It was not the bonnet, but the head that was in it," and so with Sillerton; it was not so much the locality that we should desire to place before the readers as the

13

notabilities that lived there. Once, on questioning an old crone, on the deck of an arriving Quebec liner, what part of Scotland she hailed from, the answer came without a moment's hesitation; "Sooser than Golspie, at anyhoo," Golspie being rather in proximity to John o' Groat's. Here we shall be more precise, Sillerton lay on a low valley on Donside, and in full view of the last peak of the Grampian range that overlooks the whole Buchan district, and recalls to our memory the well-known line or lines, often quoted on the east coast:

> "Tap o' Noth and Bennachie
> Are twa landmarks o' the sea."

The village occupied a central position in the parish, and was composed of about two dozen dwelling-houses, an imposing church that very probably once formed part of an ancient abbey, a good school and schoolhouse, an excellent inn, where man and beast could always command the best attention possible, and the village store, where the guid wife could exchange her butter, cheese, and eggs for those creature comforts that warm alike the outer and inner man. Add to these the meal mill, the smithy, the carpenter's and the shoemaker's workshops, and last, though not least, the famous distillery, and you have a fair picture of Sillerton. Ah! could I sweep away, as by magician's wand, half a century of years; could I summon the old villagers to return, and be as they once were, what a shaking of dry bones would be in that old churchyard! What strange groups would pass along the street; how quaint would appear their habiliments; how different from what the village man or maid may now display!

Come, let us stand at the old iron gate that separates the village of the living from the homes of the dead. Closed during the busy week, if indeed Sillerton was ever busy, it opens only on the day of rest, to admit the worshipers to the house of God, or to wander, perchance, for a brief space until the bell

proclaims the hour of prayer, wander, we say, among the
countless mounds that mark the last resting-places of departed
ones whom we never knew, and of some, too, whom we knew
right well and whose memory, yet fresh and green, may bring a
tear to the eye and sometimes, alas ! a pang to the heart.

A framed board, attached to the church wall, is eagerly
scanned by the gathering crowd, anxious to learn what matters of
public interest are there recorded for the benefit of the good folks
of Sillerton; while near by stands a stone, somewhat elevated
above the ground, on which the beadle will by and by take his
stand, at the "skailin' o' the kirk," and, in stentorian tones,
announce the coming events of importance that are on the tapis
for the week, perhaps ending with the pleasant announcement
that Jamie Uobb, the pedler, will hold a riffle of Carse o'
Gowrie apples, handkerchiefs, and tobacco, on Wednesday
evening next, at the farm of Flechneuk, and closing, very likely,
with the remark that there would be a dance after the raffle.

How strange! some will say, and this too, in Sabbath-
keeping Scotland! Ah! fifty years hence old men may be telling
to astonished listeners that they often heard ministers reading
notices from the pulpit that had long ere then found their proper
place among the advertisements of the daily or weekly
newspaper. But, hush! the bell has ceased tolling ; the wanderers
among the green mounds are hurrying nearer the church door;
while Dawvid Dunbar, the beadle, looms in sight, walking
slowly from the manse gate towards the church, and carrying in
his hand the large pulpit Bible, while behind him, with equal
pace, but with infinite dignity, rolls along the Reverend Robert
Fordyce, M. A., minister of the parish of Sillerton. The crowd
that till then had been enjoying the usual "crack," file in rapidly
as the steps of the beadle and parson draw near the iron gate, the
last to enter being a couple that had availed themselves of the
opportunity that the morning's walk afforded of whispering

murmurings of love to each other, and who now enter the sacred edifice by different doors, for, strange to say, there were at least half a dozen side doors in the church of Sillerton.

At last, all have found their places in the different seats set apart for the parishioners; the principal door is swung to upon its massive hinges; there is a moment or two of almost painful silence, and then, rising majestically in his plain but seemly pulpit, the minister of Sillerton, in slow and solemn tones, opens the service of the sanctuary in the well known phrase "Let us worship God by singing to His praise in the Hundredth Psalm."

CHAPTER III

SILLERTON AND ITS NOTABILITIES

"And the guid Culdees o' Sillerton
Might plead for King Malcolm's repose,
Wha vow'd to Sanct Andrew, their haly house,
For victory o'er his foes."

The Devil's Stane o' Kennay, slightly altered.

We were interrupted in our description of Sillerton and its surroundings by the commencement of public worship in the parish church. We shall now resume our subject, and Sillerton once properly located, as an American would probably put it, we may now proceed to sketch a few of its notabilities. There were, in those golden days, no dissenters, so called, in the parish. Had Sillerton possessed a Temple of Janus, the doors would undoubtedly have been closed, and the janitor might have safely locked them and become a Rip Van Winkle for a few years without any dread of interruption to his slumbers.

The only other place of worship, besides the parish church, was a small Episcopal chapel, once a lapidary's workshop, with a unique history of its own, but now considerably remodeled, and almost covered with ivy, and showing a Maltese cross upon either gable, as if to indicate its now sacred character. This building accommodated sufficiently a small number of the parishioners who still clung to the Episcopal form of worship, and who, along with about a dozen aristocratic families who drove there from considerable distances around, waited upon the ministrations of the Rev. William Walcott, M. A., well known for his Broad Church proclivities, an excellent scholar, an author (afterwards) of considerable notability, and who, notwithstanding all these accomplishments, had yet the good sense to preach sermons that were never known to exceed fifteen minutes in the delivery. The church of Sillerton, as has been said, was once probably part of an abbey, but the steeple, to which the church itself seemed a 'lean-to,' was of a much more ancient date, and was generally supposed to have been built by Malcolm Canmore, King of Scotland. Well it may be that Canmore was a first-class fighting man, but, judging from his attempt at building towers, he must, as an architect have proved a sad failure. We cannot, indeed, even with all our admiration for the great Malcolm, congratulate the ancient king upon the beauty of conception displayed, though certainly in durability of material used he takes the cake.

It is at least curious also that the tower of Sillerton church should have, in one respect that is to say, in the precise and exact amount of overcharge or undercharge of price for value received resembled the breeches of King Robert the Bruce. The latter were too dear, the former too cheap. Tradition has it that the king was somewhat stingy with the royal tailor as the song says:

> "In days when our King Robert rang,
> His trews they cost but half a croon ;
> He said they were a groat ower dear,
> And ca'd the tailor thief an' loon."

On the other hand, it has also been handed down that when the mason who built the tower of Sillerton had finished his work, and was on his way homewards, he looked back at the building and said, "Had I got a groat more I would have been satisfied." Groats must have been scarce in those days. Is it possible also that that dissatisfied mason had read the life of Hiram King of Tyre, who aided Solomon in his great work, and thereafter expressed anything but satisfaction with the return made by the Wise King? Being a Scotchman, and likely an Aberdonian at that, this may have well been so, and the groat too little in the case of the tower builder was much the same as the cities in Galilee that Hiram so heartily despised.

Now in attempting to describe the notabilities of Sillerton, I feel it slightly difficult to decide exactly where to begin. Are the greater or lesser lights to come first? But, as we now stand facing the tower, the puzzle seems solved by beginning at the right hand. Poor old John Laing was not much of a notability, and yet I could not consider a photo of Sillerton correct without John Laing somewhere, even though in the background. John was an elderly bachelor, and lived for many years in the village with his old mother, known in the parish by the euphonious name of Rachie Pirie. John must have been a sort of gardener in his young days, and still enjoyed the monopoly of trimming hedges, pruning trees, and of generally superintending the nurseries that supplied material for planting the waste places of Sillerton. I can imagine that I see John Laing before me now a thin, tall old man with gray hair, and clinging to the stovepipe hat that, Sunday or Saturday, he always wore.

Once he was summoned to give evidence in London before a Committee of the House of Commons in connection with some local enterprise, and what a wealth of story flowed from that little episode in his life! Not Stanley in his "Darkest Africa" could awaken interest in the breasts of his uncounted readers and admirers equal to the admiration that beamed in the faces of his youthful audience as Laing described his wonderful experiences on the round trip between Sillerton and London. The modern globe-trotter would have played only second fiddle. I would not willingly touch the truthfulness of John's reports, but deep in my memory lies the conviction that the youth of Sillerton had been taught to believe, and by one who knew it too, that the choicest dish on the Royal table, and also often the only one there was "Cream porridge and cream to them."

The occupant of the other half of Laing's house was the exciseman. Now, it generally was the case that the poor exciseman was a species of pariah of society an outcast and that were the devil to carry him away, body and bones, there would be few old wives in Scotland who would not take up the chorus of that inimitable song of Burns "We Wish you luck o' your prize, man!" In Sillerton, however, no such feeling existed; the "ewie wi' the crookit horn" had long died out, and as the gauger's duties were nearly altogether confined to the operations of the distillery his intercourse with the people generally was entirely of a social character, and in consequence he became "Good-fellow-well-met" throughout that district of the country, and was more frequently and perhaps more pleasantly employed testing the good qualities of Sillerton's usquebaugh with sugar and water than in measuring the quantities that flowed into his bonded cellars, or in tramping through moss and mire to discover some venturous Scot reaping the forbidden fruits of the little still.

I remember an adventure of the exciseman that excited no little merriment in the village. The exciseman in this instance was a family man, the husband of a thrifty wife, and the proud father of at least half a dozen bairns. It so happened that Mrs. M'Kay, in a fit of economy, suggested to her husband that their ordinary expenses would be considerably reduced were he to invest a little cash in a milch cow. The exciseman pleased, liked John Gilpin, to find that his loving spouse was possessed of a frugal mind, at once acquiesced, and as there was a 'roup' at the farm of Xethermains the following week, it was decided that on that eventful day the ganger should proceed thither, and that if cows were sold for anything like feasible prices, he should become the purchaser of one, and at once bring his prize home with him. On the day of sale the exciseman sallied forth accordingly to purchase the coveted cow. Thegauger, however, no matter how competent he might be to tell the quantity and quality of a cask of whisky, felt that, in gauging the qualities of a cow, he was somewhat at sea, and so, after obtaining the opinion of two or three cronies, and treating each expert in the usual way, he himself got about half seas over; the advice or advices he had received got considerably mixed; and the result was somewhat different from what he intended, and from what his better half had desired. Somewhere among the small hours the honest but fuddled gauger might have been seen leading a quadruped into the byre that had been prepared beforehand for the purchase, but as every member of his family had long ere then gone to sleep, it devolved upon Mr. M'Kay to make his cow comfortable for the night.

Somewhat later on his better half learned that the cow was awaiting her attention, and, armed with the ordinary milking pail, she proceeded to business. The result was almost fatal to Her Majesty's collector of Excise. A quadruped was in the stable, but, alas! the bovine characteristics were entirely wanting: the obfuscated ganger had, instead of a cow, bought a horse.

The wrath of Mrs. M'Kay needed no nursing to keep it warm; it attained incandescent heat at oncE; and the hapless exciseman! how did he fare? Well, I would prefer not to penetrate too deeply into the secrets of any man's fireside, but this I may say, that if little milk came from the byre, there was a corresponding scarcity of the milk of human kindness everywhere about the ganger's surroundings for some time. The wags of Sillerton did not readily forget the oft-told story of the exciseman leading home by a halter his so-called cow.

CHAPTER IV

THE DOMINIE

"And still the wonder grew
That one small head should carry all he knew."

Goldsmith.

In the tall house on the opposite side of the gate lived the Reverend Louis Alexander Daff, M. A., the parish schoolmaster. At the time I first recollect the Reverend Louis, he had retired from some of the duties of active life, and, in consequence, employed an assistant, who attended to parochial duties, while he himself enjoyed the major part of the revenue that made the parish schoolmaster an envied man. But, notwithstanding that the old dominie had not, for several years, wielded the taws in training the young ideas of Sillerton how to shoot, yet his history was peculiarly green in the memories of his contemporaries, and how often has the writer of this listened to the quaint stories of his life, and the peculiar traits of character that he had shown during an incumbency that had exceeded half a century!

Could we but hear the village worthies, as they gathered in the smithy on certain occasions, or while they crowded the merchant's shop on a Saturday evening, telling anecdotes of the old pedagogue, it would be a treat that Max O'Rell himself might long to enjoy. "Weel, he may be a very douce man noo, but, by my certie, he wisna aye that," and so out the story came, among many others, of how Louis preached his first sermon at Sillerton; in fact, this is a species of Scottish bull, seeing that on the occasion alluded to, when Louis certainly should have preached, Louis did not preach at all. We may just here state, for information's sake, that the parish school was frequently the first rung of the ladder that led to the parish church, and the incumbent of the school of Sillerton, in his youth, aimed, like most other dominies, at not only "shakin' his head in a pu'pit," but at exchanging the ferula of authority that he wielded for some cozy parish church nay, perhaps for that of Sillerton itself, which his father then occupied, and who, under ordinary circumstances, might betimes require an assistant and successor.

The old minister, therefore, was as anxious as his son that the latter should become, as soon as possible, a licensed preacher of the Gospel, and thus a fit candidate for any pastoral charge that might offer. The ordinary sessions had been taken at the Divinity Hall, the ordinary examinations had been undergone by the candidate for church patronage, and after the last, Louis Alexander was licensed by the Presbytery to preach the Gospel, the Presbytery leaving it to the licentiate to choose some church, within the bounds, where his first sermon should be preached.

Now, there was no little delicacy here. In your native parish where you had fooled with most of the young men, both in school and college days, and where, perhaps, you might have made love to a few of the prettiest maidens and there was truly no lack of that commodity either in the village or in the parish it was no easy matter for a participant in all these vanities to cast off at once the old slough of worldly-mindedness, trip up gaily the pulpit stairs, and become at once the monitor, nay perchance, the judge, of those who had formerly (ah! how short a time ago) joined in his folly. But Louis Alexander had been somewhat a sly dog, and his old father had no knowledge of anything whatever that might have brought the faintest blush to the young dominie's cheek, as he entered, for the first time, his father's pulpit. I do not exactly know what Louis' feelings were on that eventful Saturday that preceded the day when he was, by his father's special request, to hold forth to the parishioners of Sillerton. Days, nay, nights as well, had been spent in his preparations; his

23

carefully-conned sermon had received its final touches; the other parts of the service had also received due attention, and nothing remained but that the actual performance should be in keeping with the successful rehearsal. Yet, notwithstanding all the preparations, Louis Alexander was not a particularly happy man on that eventful Saturday.

The work of the forenoon in the school engaged his attention for some time, but as Saturday was a half-holiday in Scotland even in those early days, the vacant afternoon left Daff considerably too much time to think over the trying ordeal that awaited him in his father's pulpit the next day. Evening came at last, and after a hurried tea, partaken of very sparingly by the embryo preacher, he retired to his own room, leaving orders that he should not be disturbed till breakfast time the following morning. Gradually the shop and smithy poured forth their respective groups of honest plowmen that dropped in at the village on a Saturday night to get a sock sharpened, or perhaps to purchase an ounce or two of good twist tobacco; maybe to get a glimpse of some bonnie lassie that found it necessary to search around for a seemly peat wherewith to 'rest' her fire for the night, for mind you those were yet scarcely the days of Lucifer matches. Well, strange though it may seem, yet it invariably happened on these Saturday nights, when curfew time came, Jenny had difficulty in finding a suitable peat, and just as she was almost giving up the task in despair, Jocky chanced mark you, 'chanced' to put in an appearance; the peat was soon found, for the youth was a good judge of these articles; the fire was speedily 'rested,' and Jocky was I had almost said, soon on his way homewards. There is no doubt this should have been the case, for the guidman and his help meet had long retired to the privacy of their own chamber, but somehow or other there was a difficulty in saying 'goodnight.' No, there was no difficulty in saying 'good-night,' but in saying the very last 'goodnight.' Othello knew something of this when he said, 'One more, and this the last.' I believe that the Sillerton youths of that day had some idea that 'good-night' was a species of adjective that had the ordinary, perhaps extraordinary, degrees of comparison. It went with them, apparently, through the positive, comparative and superlative degrees, but for some reason, that has never been fully explained, the superlative 'good-night' seemed the hardest nut to crack in the lover's grammar. Certainly it was no noun, for it never seemed to be declined, and though those years have drifted far away, yet I have a most vivid recollection of the almost insurmountable difficulties that were sometimes encountered before the lips could be framed to utter honestly that is, without equivocation or mental reservation of any kind whatever that last that very last 'goodnight.' Sillerton was soon still as the grave. As Peter Pindar says somewhere:

> "Now silence in the country stalk'd the dews,
> As if she wore a flannel pair of shoes,
> Lone list'ning, as the poets well remark,
> To falling mill-streams and the mastiff's bark;
> To loves of wide-mouth'd cats, most mournful tales;
> To hoot of owls amid the dusky vales."

The last candle in the manse had passed beneath the extinguisher; the last shell lamp in the village had died out, and Louis Alexander Daff, the parish schoolmaster, and the aspirant for ecclesiastical honors, is supposed to have yielded to nature's sweet restorer sleep. And now comes in a small additional portion of the story as it was told. Well, as to Louis, we shall see. Morning came; breakfast came also to the occupants of the manse; but Louis Alexander came not. The father was somewhat troubled at the non-appearance of his son, and a maidservant was detailed to summon the loiterer to partake of that substantial Scotch meal that in old-world homes was the meal of the day, but no Louis was there; the sheets were cold the bird had flown.

CHAPTER V

THE DOMINIE, CONTINUED

"Gie him strong drink until he wink,
That's sinking in despair;
And liquor guid to fire his bluid,
That's press'd wi' grief and care :
There let him bouse, an' deep carouse,
Wi' bumpers flowing o'er,
Till he forgets his loves or debts,
An' minds his grief, no more."

Proverbs, xxxi., 6,7

In the last chapter it was said that the ambitious Dominie had retired to his own room. Bat, alas! there was no rest there for him. Thoughts of next day's duties weighed heavily on his mind, and instead of seeking a cessation of his troubles beneath the blankets, Daff slid quietly down from his bedroom window, and sauntered leisurely along the village road. What he intended to do or where he intended to go, as he slipped that night from his window, I am unable to say. Probably he thought that a quiet daunder would cool his blood, and predispose him that sleep that would give him the respite of at least a few hours. At length, however, his steps somehow turned in the direction of Paradise, a species of Oriental garden that graced one of the many beautiful meadows of Sillerton, and where the chief gardener was a crony of the schoolmaster. Daft' was wont to drop in occasionally there, and generally before leaving there was produced a drop of good Scotch whisky, just for auld lang syne, in accordance with the habit and custom in those days. But, out of respect to Mr. Daffs character, we must say right here that he was universally known us a strictly temperate man, and if his conduct that Saturday night was riot precisely what it should be, yet, if fall he did, he fell like better folk in Paradise, and that the weakness which on that occasion humbled him was never again, even through a long lifetime, repeated. John Tamson, the chief gardener, on the other hand, was what the folk thereabouts called a drouthy bodie. He was given to what were known as 'spates,' and on those occasions, we fear, neglected his duties as the chief custodian of Paradise, and incensed accordingly his employer, Sir Archibald Gamut, the old laird. Nay, it was known that on one occasion Sir Archibald had, in great wrath, dismissed his old servant, and had, there and then, ordered him to look out for another place.

The somewhat noisy sorrow of Tarnson made a very evident impression on his old master, who, perhaps, in some degree relenting, demanded if he had anything to say in his own behalf that might stay the execution of the sentence that had been pronounced against him, One peculiarity of Tamson was that while his limbs, under the influence of innumerable glasses of whisky, refused to be in any way directed by the will of their owner, in fact produced what might have been called a 'locomotive strike,' yet the headpiece seemed to soar above such petty weakness, and tongue and brain kept clear and cool as ever. It has been said that this gift, if it might be so called, was not confined to John Tamson, but was a peculiarity of the folks of Sillerton, although it has been said also to be common to most Scotchmen, and in fact it has been not only whispered but even printed, too, that an honest Scotch parson, after a whole evening spent in recuperating an exhausted frame, had been heard to say that he was 'michtily refreshed,' the refreshment indicated on this occasion being only thirteen tumblers of toddy.

Well, as to John Tamson, his limbs were fairly out of order, but with a spade in one hand, and a good grip of a yew tree, under which the laird and he were standing, he was just able to articulate a plagiarized verse of one the Psalrns of David, and parodied too at that:

> "How lovely is thy dwelling-place,
> Sir Ar-chi-bald, to me;
> The graveled walks of Paradise,
> Their like I'll never see."

When the old man reached the word 'never' he became deeply moved. Had he been playing on a modern organ then, he would probably have touched the stop marked 'Tremulante,' but as his extemporized music was entirely vocal, it seemed as if he would never stop, and when he reached the final 'see,' his performance degenerated into a note that was not precisely a whine, and yet not particularly different from a genuine howl. The words and music, however, produced a softening influence upon the good laird; his savage breast was soothed, and with a hearty roar of laughter, John Tamson's sentence was revoked, and he was relegated once more to delve about the graveled walks of Paradise.

Such was Louis Alexander Daff's host on that memorable Saturday night. The schoolmaster's story was soon told. The old-fashioned bine bottle duly made its appearance. A few glasses of the generous, soothing liquor found its way to the very heart of the troubled Dominie, till, alas! the truth must be confessed, poor Daff was overtaken, and some time among the sma' hours he fell into a profound sleep. At the time good old Daff was filling what should have been that day his son's place in the pulpit of Sillerton, that son was still slumbering peacefully on the bed of John Tamson, in Paradise, for "Partly wi' fear he was o'ercome, And partly he was drunk, that night." A gentle whisper reached the manse, during the afternoon, of the whereabouts of Louis Alexander, and as the gloamin' deepened into the darkness of a quiet Sunday summer evening, the minister's gig deposited near the manse door the considerably shaken-up person of the still obfuscated schoolmaster. Quietly he stole away to his own room without obtruding his company upon his irate father. Sleep speedily came to restore an equilibrium that had been sadly disturbed amid the groves of Paradise, and as the sun sent his first rays over the parish of Sillerton, and lighted up the heath-clad face of the distant Bennachie, the would-be preacher awoke to commence his duties of the week awoke perhaps a sadder, but certainly a wiser man.

CHAPTER VI

THE DOMINIE MOUNTED

"So stooping clown, as needs he must
Who cannot sit upright,
He grasp'd the mane with both his hands,
And eke with all his might."

John Gilpin.

One other tale of the old Dominie that never failed to awaken the merriment of the listeners was connected with his horsemanship, which, very evidently, was not of a remarkably high order. It was just possible though that the schoolmaster had but few opportunities of studying the noble art of equestrianism. Occasionally, like some eccentric comet, the great and famous Ord appeared on the Sillerton horizon, to show off his splendid bareback riding and feats of horsemanship; yet only a few boys attempted to imitate him, and of all men in the world Louis Alexander would have been the last to follow the example. It was also true that the eccentric Earl of Kintore occasionally rode through the village with his huntsmen and hounds, and there were shown places where he had made tremendous leaps in pursuit of reynard, but these saltations the douce dominie would scarcely have attempted had even Tarn o' Shanter's carlin been behind him.

Bold Buffalo Bill was then a name unknown, and cowboys had not as yet been evolved from the quiet Scotch herd laddie, nor, in consequence, had their feats on Mexican plugs or bucking mustangs been exhibited in all their glory to awaken the admiration or excite the rivalry of the British equestrian. Without much schooling in the equinal mysteries, therefore, Daff took kindly to a horse probably in this way. During his more youthful days, when juvenile ambition fills the human heart with the intense desire of doing something that might call down the praises of our fellow-men, he might have pleaded guilty to the soft impeachment. Many men at that age become imbued with martial ardor; feel that there is that in them that might some day convert them into Napoleons or Wellingtons; sigh for a life of glory, and leaving kirk, or school, or farm behind, join the ranks of those who seek the 'bubble reputation at the cannon's mouth.' Well, Louis was not one of those. Another man is fired by tales of travel and adventure by sea and land, and the mantle of Mungo Park: falls on his shoulders, and the next thing we hear of him is he is hunting buffalo with Blackfeet Indians on the western prairies of America, or listening to an original negro melody at the sources of the Nile.

Ah! no; Louis' affections did not incline in that direction. In fact, to come to the point, his love of discovery or adventure did not spur him on far to the eastward or westward of the boundary line of the parish of Sillerton. The ambition of Daff, such as it was, was circumscribed. That ambition, though deferred for several years, was to possess a horse, and to exhibit his figure upon that quadruped's back every afternoon as far as the farm of Scrapehard, and back again to the schoolhouse of Sillerton. This he had done for over a year, week in and week out, wind and rain (there was no tide in Sillerton, barring a few holiday tides that were still remembered) wind and rain we said permitting, for no man was more careful of his health than the schoolmaster of Sillerton. It was observed, however, that he dominie never once during this time had brought his equestrian exercises to a pace faster than an ordinary walk. The trot, the canter, and the gallop were utterly ignored, and had the feelings of man and beast been subjected to the operations of a mind-reader, it might have been hard to decide, to which the slow, tranquil pace was the more pleasing. But hereby hangs a tale.

Doctor Low, the village medical practitioner, had exercised his profession for some time in the district, for a doctor's field of practice in those days extended frequently over several parishes, and was bounded only by his reputation, and the ability of his nag to carry him over the long rides that he was often required to undertake. Low was, without question, a harum-scarum, a reckless horseman, and, for some reason unexplained, no admirer of the douce schoolmaster.

In Low's mind a suspicion had arisen why Daff's equestrian exercises had never exceeded the simplest movement, and overtaking him one day, just as lie had turned his horse's head homeward, the mad doctor at once proceeded to test the accuracy of his suspicions. Slipping up quietly, on his nag, behind the unsuspecting Dominie, the doctor dealt Dobbin a terrible cut with his whip over the hind-quarters. The effect was electrical. Unused to such treatment, the astonished brute threw his hind heels in the air, and at a thundering gallop made for the village as if something worse than a nest of hornets was behind him. That whip-cut also produced a very extraordinary effect upon the horseman. His seat was naturally anything but a good one, even at his usual pace, but hen, without any preliminaries, the quiet, sedate walk became a terrific, thundering gallop, that seat was nowhere, or rather the seat was everywhere, now up about a foot and a half above the snorting horse, now bumped with the force of a sledge-hammer against the crupper of his saddle, and now and again changing sides, till the poor pedagogue seemed as if describing circles round a movable center, that center being somewhere along the spinal cord of his bounding steed.

Louis Alexander's mind, however, never lost entirely its equilibrium no matter how much that of his body was disturbed. Danger he certainly felt, but self-preservation was an inherent principle of his nature, and doing just what he was only able to do, and in this following the commendable example of the "Train-band captain of famous London Town," under somewhat similar circumstances, he leaned forward upon his horse's neck, left the flowing reins to the guiding hand of chance, if to nothing better, and, with hands desperately entwined among the exuberant tresses of Dobbin's mane, bade fair at first to leave his tormentor behind him. But, alas! such was not to be; the village doctor was better mounted than the parish Dominie; the one nag was a fiery steed, accustomed to respond to his rider's importunities, while poor Dobbin, even had all other things been equal, was sadly handicapped, and so it came to pass that both riders entered the astonished village, not exactly neck and neck, but Daff leading by a length. The whole village man, woman, and child (there were no canines in Sillerton) turned out to see what the noise meant, for the triumphant medico never missed a thwack of his whip, nor a tally-ho of his tongue, till the sair-forfoughten Dominie found shelter within his own gates. There was not much law then in Sillerton; that was a luxury for the great ones of the earth, and actions for assault and battery were there utterly unknown. Sillerton, in fact, in this proved that history often repeats itself, for an ancient heathen poet says in words that, freely translated into English, would give the stanza as under:

> "By love of right, and native justice led,
> In straight paths of equity they tread;
> Nor know the bar, nor fear the judge's frown,
> Unpractis'd in the wranglings of the gown."

The sufferer had simply to grin and bear, and the poor schoolmaster, on account of the many bruises sustained by his lower limbs, was said to have worn something resembling a kilt for ten days thereafter, till the skin wounds were gradually and effectually healed, though some mental and even physical scars may have doubtless remained. The village worthies delighted to tell this tale when rent-day and cracks and ale came round; and wicked Low, it was believed, never repented of what he had done, and continued, for many a year afterwards, to crack his whip and his jokes merrily as ever.

A change, however, had come over the spirit of his victim's dream ; his ambition, if ambition it was, had to find vent in some other and safer channel; and the saddle and spurs, like the warrior's disused weapons, thereafter hung idly in the hall of the schoolhouse. Louis Alexander Daff never mounted steed again.

CHAPTER VII

A DISSOLVING VIEW

"The knights are dust ; their swords are rust ;
Their souls are with the saints we trust."

It appears to the author of this simple yet authentic narrative as if he had determined in his own mind to write nothing about the folks of Sillerton but what might excite only our risible faculties. Now, this charge, if charge it is, we are inclined to explain, if not indeed to deny. There might have been, and there doubtless were, many things that happened in the village and its surroundings in those boyhood days of ours that were well calculated to stir our better nature to its profoundest depths; there were tragedies enacted there that perhaps sent the dagger of sorrow as straight to the heart as when the guileless Desdemona died beneath the hand of the loving but jealous Moor; there were pages of remorse written there on the stricken soul that no pen shall ever chronicle; tears shed that were felt only by the cheeks over which they flowed, and blighted hopes there were, that death, in summer's prime, might only faintly indicate; but in life the silent lips kept their secret well, arid now the humble, moss-grown tombstone tells no tales. Some things of a saddened character certainly happened occasionally in Sillerton, and were perhaps known and felt by us also, but the tear and sigh were soon forgotten by the young, for to them the clouds return not after the rain; it was the laughter of the merry that still and ever kept ringing in our ears. And so, when much of the grave and sad has been washed away from memory by the waves of time, the merry things that happened, and the quaint and jocular stories that were told, made deeper tracks in our memories, and in consequence yet linger round us still, and rise up before us as if the wand of some mighty magician had called them all back to new-born life and action. Well, there is nothing particularly merry before us at the present moment; there may, however, be something pleasant to contemplate, and hence enjoyable. Louis Alexander Daff not he of youthful days nor he of robust manhood, but Daff the now superannuated schoolmaster of Sillerton, still claims a few pages of notice ere he pass by to mingle with the shadows of the past.

I can now see before me that old man, of whom I have already said so much, weaned of the frivolities of youth, few as they were, and descending into the vale of years, surrounded by the respect of his neighbors, and bearing along with him the hallowed privileges and dignities of age. He still enjoys his outing, but the saddle has long given place to the more sober social gig; Dobbin, the third in succession of that name, gray like his master, walks along in harness, and Mrs. Daff, kindly and homely in all her ways, is always beside her loving lord as he drives save the mark! back and forth between the eighteenth milestone and the schoolhouse of Sillerton. Just at this point in my narrative, however candor compels me to say something of my own connection with the Dominie's stable arrangements, and should the laugh be turned against me, as it certainly has every chance of being, it must at least be borne in mind that a barefooted callant on horseback is very apt to ride pretty much towards the same destination which beggars under similar conditions are said to reach. It might help also to break my own fall considerably to remind the reader that "he rides siccar that never faas."

It may be as well also to mention that Daff kept no man or boy to look after outside affairs. A few ays of a handy laborer sufficed to plant the kail and potatoes in spring, and to house them when autumn came. In fact the servant girl was a maid of all work; looked pretty much after the nag, and faithfully bestowed upon the animal the daily allowance of oats and hay that Louis Alexander gave. Beyond, however, the feeding, Kirsty did no more, and to her the mysteries of curry-comb arid brush were absolutely unknown. The truth was that had not Daff been equal to the occasion, a modern Hercules would have speedily been required to clean the Dominie's stable. But to fend off such a dilemma, Daff, cunning old rogue that he was, had succeeded in associating the brushing of Dobbin with the highest honors.

Daily for a few minutes the old man entered the schoolroom to exchange greetings with his assistant, and to inquire particularly how the Latinists were getting on. After exhorting the latter to study well and faithfully the rudiments, adding very emphatically on every occasion, "The rudiments are the very soul of the language," he detailed two of our number Latinists, always Latinists to brush up Dobbin FG the afternoon's drive. I had often been one of the two detailed for fatigue duty, if fatigue it could be called, for the loose hairs on Dobbin were more likely to be rubbed off by our corduroy breeches than by the regulation curry-comb. The fact was that after a very small amount of rubbing down we were accustomed to take the old horse out of the stable, and with one boy on his back and another in the rear armed with a good whip, we had lively times of it, and doubtless refreshed our own memories of a former Dobbin's youthful gallop, with mad Doctor Low behind him. The pig, however, goes to the well till one day, and so with me and my stolen rides. My turn had now come, for my comrade was down, and I was 'up.', 'Boots and saddles' had sounded, or in this case rather 'Boots and no saddies,' and with two or three smart cuts received from the whip, Dobbin seemed as if he would break the record. A shower had, however, rendered the race-course dangerously slippery, and just as my gallant steed turned the corner of the hen-house our winning post man and horse came heavily to the ground. No doubt a feeling of fear crossed my mind at that supreme moment, not knowing exactly what the consequences of the tumble might be.

SCOTTISH FOLKLORE

Dr. Livingstone, the great African missionary and explorer, describes his sensations under the operating teeth of an angry lion, and concludes, from personal experience, that the rat in the clutches of his natural enemy receives a sudden shock to his nervous system that banishes both fear and suffering, and renders death almost, if not altogether, painless. This is doubtless true, but true it is also that a greater danger seems to entirely supersede a lesser one. And so in my case. In the act of falling I was sensible of the imminent danger to life and limb, but just then I caught a glimpse of the face of the thunderstruck and irate old man glaring ominously at me over the school fence. For once in my life I played fox and lay still. The old horse, with sundry wriggles and struggles and groans, found his legs again, but I deemed it more expedient not to find mine. Instantaneously the wrath of old Duff disappeared in the stronger feeling of fear lest one of his beloved Latinists had been rendered hors de combat, and with kindly hands I was lifted up. My aute-morteni statement was at once taken. It was found, or at least surmised, that I was not mortally wounded. No bones were broken, so far at least as Duff's very limited anatomical knowledge might venture on an opinion. But, from the dreadful limp that at once developed, it was plain that I must be hurt somewhere. A few kindly words, however, brought back the color to my cheek, and as I expressed an ability and wish to return at once to my placa among the Latinists, the fears of the Dominie at once vanished, and with a little assistance I was soon in the schoolroom and at work again. I received no scolding whatever, and my comrade, who was clearly particeps criminis, or 'airt and pairt' as we express it in Scotch, got off as well. There were sly looks as we both sat down in our places in the schoolroom to scan a few lines in Virgil, the lesson for the afternoon, and the assistant teacher, who somehow, probably from information received from Daff himself, seemed to take in the situation, could not resist the temptation of quizzing us by showing the onomatopoetic beauties of the very appropriate line, Quadrupedante putrem sotiitu quatit unyida campum. Personally we did not enjoy the joke. Sore bones, and bruised muscles, and the abrasion of a few square inches of cuticle on one's person are not generally accompanied by very marked demonstrations of hilarity; and then, over and above all this, we had mental wounds as well to endure, we knew and felt that we had lost our spurs, curry combs and stolen gallops were no more for us, we were reduced to the rank of infantry soldiers, and like good old Daff himself in years gone by, dismounted for another reason forever we had had our last ride on Dobbin. It was more, however, to depict the kindlier feelings of the village Dominie that this chapter was begun than to immortalize my own exploits, may I not simply say failures? Gladly I draw a veil over this youthful escapade, and direct your eyes to a more pleasing spectacle.

Come, then, and let us take our place beside the pump that stands exactly in the middle of the tree-shaded square. The original founder of Sillerton had evidently been a mathematician, and, with a colossal pair of compasses in his hand, stuck one point down in the center, saying, "Here is the well," and with a radius of a considerable number of yards, swung the other leg around till the circle was complete. Round that circumference a hedge of hawthorn and beech was planted, while elm and ash trees filled the inside of the circle. One bisecting line passed through this, terminating towards one end in the door of the inn, and towards the other in the great door of the church, and affording thus on either side an easy access to the water supply for the villagers.

Round this circle ran a well-kept road, and completing it there were four rows of houses forming a rectangle rather than an exact square. The trees rose to a considerable height, and opposite to the schoolhouse a mighty elm threw out a giant arm as if to exchange courtesies with the old schoolmaster. The steeple clock has just struck nine, but scarcely has the last stroke sounded when a window opens; a night-capped head looks out, a kindly hand strews an abundance of crumbs upon the window-sill; a low whistle is heard, and in an instant the hoary elm is alive with birds. Roderick Dim's whistle brought stalwart warriors innumerable from rock and tree and bracken bush, but Daff's quiet signal summons countless songsters, apparently from earth and heaven. The beautiful goldfinch is there; the more somber chaffinch; the brilliant bullfinch; the homely but songful siskin, while a whole army at least of robin redbreasts assert their claim to human sympathy a claim also never disputed; while a considerable colony of overbearing, pugnacious, and ubiquitous sparrows all haste into that window-sill to share in a breakfast that, Saturday and Sunday, summer and winter, is never forgotten.

Later on in the day, as the old man sits in the playground upon his easy-chair, we bring our pets to receive his praise, and a more tangible acknowledgment at the same time, and also to hear his oft repeated admonition; "Be kind, boys, to the lower animals." We would almost wish to stop here, but no; the whole truth must needs be told, arid there are still in Sillerton men who as boys stood on that playground beside the schoolmaster, as he dispensed his praise and his pence to those who had treated his pets with kindness, and who will perhaps recollect that we did not always act on the square with the old man.

Poor Daff's eyesight had got dim, and his affection for birds and beasts was infinitely stronger than his memory. And did we not play upon these frailties? Did not the jackdaw, that, five minutes ago belonged to Jack, become in an instant the property of Gill, and that, too, by a sleight of hand that might have done credit to the "Great Wizard of the North"; and had we not frequently to hustle round to find new recruits for pay-day parade to supply the places of those who had all died in the meantime? This was very naughty on our part, but at all events, no matter our merits or demerits, Louis Alexander tried, in good faith, by rewards, to stimulate the young folks to exercise forbearance and kindliness towards the lower animals, and even if only too often his method of inculcating kindness was abused, yet still it ceased not to bear fruit.

How often have we been indebted to little incidents that happened to us in childhood for some of thos tastes that thereafter grew with our growth until they influenced our whole lives, and sometimes we could scarcely tell how they originated with us! Personally I owe much to the simple alphabet of natural history that the old teacher taught me on the playground of Sillerton. On the playgreen of Sillerton there was little taught of the natural history of science, but there was much of that natural history with which the kindlier feelings of the heart have to do. We certainly learned but little there of the great classes into which the animal kingdom was divided; orders, families, genera, species, and varieties were not household words with the kindly schoolmaster, but if watching a ruby-throated humming bird sipping its nectar and drawing its other supplies from the storehouse of a flower, or listening to the newly arrived Canadian rossignol pouring forth its sweet song, long ere the March winds had ceased to blow if these are pleasures that I have been privileged to enjoy, how much of that enjoyment owed its very existence to the suggestive example of the kind Dominie; and the oft-repeated maxim, spoken on the schoolgreen of Sillerton, so many long years ago, still whispers in my ear, even amid the solitudes of the primeval forest, "Boys, be kind to the lower animals." We owe this tribute, and we pay it willingly, to the memory of the kind old man. The end came calmly as the quiet of a summer gloaming. The birds, as their wont was, flocked to the unopened window, but no breakfast awaited them that morning; the hands that had long dispensed the crumbs to those that neither sow nor reap were folded in rest; the heart that had so often sent forth its warm sympathies to the lower formations of the Creator's hand was cold and still, there was indeed a vacancy not only in the school of Sillerton, but in its village square as well ; the fluttering and twittering of the little winged orphans around the unopened schoolhouse window, and the absence of the well-known white nightcap, were the first intimation to the villagers that their kindly neighbor would never again feed and clothe the poor, nor scatter crumbs to the little songsters that were still awaiting him at the draped window; and soon all that was mortal of the Rev. Louis Alexander Dan was laid to rest beside his kindred dust in the old churchyard.

After the funeral, a few friends gathered in the schoolhouse, as was the custom, to hear the will read. Daff had been a careful man, and left behind him a considerable amount of worldly wealth. Due provision was therefore made for the sorrowing widow; and, true to his character, among the legacies there was a weekly allowance set apart for Dobbin, and an annual dole set aside also for the board of a favorite cock, these sums to be paid during the natural term of their lives. Strange to say, twenty years thereafter old Dobbin was still to be seen on the braes of Fetternear, and that identical cock was still crowing then, as if, like the eagles, he had renewed his age.

Did a superabundance of kindly care keep the legatees in life? Did the caretaker of these two happy orphans discover and administer to his wards some elixir of life that enabled them to enjoy the bounty of their departed master long after the period usually allotted to the equine or the gallinaceous animals; or was it possible, as some miserable misanthropes hinted, that old Dobbin and his ancient comrade had long ago ceased to neigh and crow, but that fit representatives had been found to enjoy that bounty that the village schoolmaster bestowed upon at least two of the lower animals in his hist will and testament?

With the old squire we might say, "Much might be said

on both sides." and

"He prayeth best who loveth best
All things both great and small;
For the dear God who loveth us,
He made and loveth all."

CHAPTER VIII

THE STICKIT LAWYER

"The poor inhabitant below
Was quick to learn and wise to know,
And keenly felt the friendly glow
And softer flame;
But thoughtless follies laid him low,
And stain'd his name."

The Bard's Epitaph.

We have looked into the hist will and testament of Lotus Alexander Duff, whose tombstone still adorns the quiet churchyard of Sillerton; but ere "we draw the curtain down," we would fain point out one other scene in this connection, so to speak, and touch, it may be but lightly, upon the other members of the Daft' family. There is little to be said of them, but yet that little seems necessary to till up and render complete, as it were, the background. Two maiden sisters and a ne'er-do-well brother, Sandy, complete the group. Sandy was certainly an M. A. of Aberdeen, as we shall see or hear, it may be, by and by, but he attained the position of only a stickit lawyer, and reached no higher. Some small provision had been made for the two old maids, and with assiduous care they were able to keep a roof over their heads in a neighboring parish; the said roof also, though of heather, sheltered as well poor spendthrift Sandy. Their brother the schoolmaster died in the spring, and as the appointment of a successor would not take place for some little time, a considerate friend, the very reference to whom brings a tear to my eye, suggested that it would be a work of charity to put in a crop in the dead man's garden for the benefit of the living members of the family. This was quietly accomplished.

The left hand, in this case, did not know what the right hand had done. Potatoes had been planted in the old monks' garden; a reasonable amount of labor had been bestowed upon them, and when the autumn came the increase seemed to have become at least thirty-fold. I was then a stripling attending a neighboring school, and passing every day the door of the Daff family. It was now necessary to inform them what had been done, and I had received a suitable message, though it might have been altered in my mind and memory as I hurried on to school. I knocked at the humble door as directed, and instantly two thin, worn, ancient maidens stood before me, and rather curtly demanded my business.

Somewhat confused, I blurted out "The taties are ready for houkin' in the schoolyard o' Sillerton, and your brither Sandy better gae up and look after them." Ye gods! what a scraich greeted me. "Sandy! What Sandy dae ye mean? Sandy! Sandy! Sandy!" rising in the inflection till the last 'Sandy' reached a note that I have never since heard, even through the trained lips of a pri madonna. "Ye aiblins mean Maister Alexander Daff, our brither. He is nae Sandy, but a Maister o' Airts of Aberdeen, for weel-a-wat our father paid good siller for the honor Sandy, did ye say?" But I had heard and seen enough; a species of terror now added wings to my feet, and I heard no more. The Master of Arts, however, Sandy or no Sandy, duly put in an appearance, and the potatoes that grew in the school-house garden of Sillerton were boiled by the maiden sisters of the Master of Arts. I remember well one of Sandy's tricks. Fond of a little tobacco was he, but seldom was he able to indulge in that luxury. Fortune, however, on one occasion at least, deigned to favor him. A sad influx of caterpillars came, the berry bushes were in imminent danger, and tobacco smoke alone could put to flight the enemy. Poor Sandy for once in his life was happy. The ill wind blew him good on this occasion. His sisters purchased a few ounces of twist; a pipe was procured, no matter where, and I had several times the pleasure of seeing the Master of Arts smoking away contentedly the pests that threatened to bring ruin upon his sisters' gooseberries.

A whole week was spent in the conscientious performance of duty, and had the sisters' purse held out, Sandy Daff would have smoked on, without one grumble at the trouble it cost him, till the berries were falling from the bushes, or to hitter Lammas for aught I know.

One incident more I shall relate to fill up the background I have attempted to paint, and we shall then finish with the Daff family. Sandy was fond of tobacco, but Sandy was also fond of whisky. Hence those tears! hence the stickit lawyer! hence a misspent life, and smoking vile tobacco beneath a gooseberry bush, when instead, arrayed in silken gown, he should have been reaping a golden harvest at the bar. But such, alas! Was not for Sandy. Occasionally he reached Sillerton on Saturday evening, but for what purpose it were hard to say. Long habit, may have made the journey chronic, if journeys ever become so, but the chance of a drop of the barley bree was inducement enough to him to walk a few miles on the pleasures of hope. One Saturday evening he had, for probably good cause, been turned out of the village shop. Sandy bent to the inevitable, but lie recollected and winced under the insult. In those primitive days a monthly market was held in the town of Inverurie, and there congregated business men from every surrounding district. Sandy was waiting and watching for his revenge.

Down, next market day, came slowly about a dozen riders from Sillerton. They must needs pass very close to Duff's humble dwelling. As they approached, the Master of Arts rushed forward to meet them, stood on the highway, and most obsequiously lifted his hat to the shopkeeper, who was one of the party, and who, little more then a week before, had turned him out of his store. Pleased by Sandy's attention, Baggs, who was a vain man, drew up his nag, and addressed his respectful friend. This was just what and all that Sandy wanted. Emitting a series of sounds that were admirably adapted to express his contempt, he turned away hastily on his heel, muttering loud enough to be heard by all the party "Excuse me, sir; I mistook you for a gentleman." If the scowl that came from one, and the roar of laughter that rose from all the rest were worth anything, Sandy had won a sweet revenge. Not very long after, that small building was tenantless the two sisters had passed away and the schoolmaster's brother, Sandy Daff, the Aberdeen Master of Arts, soon followed. In him death gleaned the last sheaf of the Daff family. Alas! poor Yorick!

CHAPTER IX

DOCTOR LOW'S WATCH LOST AND FOUND

"Ye ken Jock Hornbook i' the clachan,
Deil mak' his king's-hood in a spleuchan;
He's grown sae weel acquaint wi' Buchan
An' ither chaps,
The weans had oot their fingers laughin',
An' pouk my hips."

Burns.

Doctor Low had in youthful, palmy days accelerated the movements of young Dobbin and his canny master from Nethermains to the village of Sillerton. But this was many years before I knew Sillerton, and it was only the old stories that I heard. But I also knew Low. In a small 'fell' biggin', in somewhat advanced age, and alone, lived the old doctor. But Low's occupation was gone. The places that knew him once now knew him no more. New kings had risen that knew not Joseph. Young science had made strides that left the old practitioner behind. Like the old three-deckers whose last shot had been fired, and which now, giving place to the ironclads of a recent day, lay stranded, useless hulks upon the shore, so a younger and better educated class of medicals had come in to place their predecessors high and dry upon the shelf; and the old practitioners, if they had failed to provide something for a rainy day, now sank into abject poverty, or depended upon the charity of one or two who enabled them to live without knowing that they were actual paupers. Such, alas! was poor old Low. Times had gone hard with the old man. Ah! could he have lived upon the stories about himself that the writer of this has listened to, he would have died of obesity. And such stories, too! Our grandfathers, and grandmothers also, had a plain way of talking, and told tales in the drawing-room that could not now be whispered in the kitchen, for the modern cook would blush at the recital and the pretty housemaid would play bopeep through her fingers, and declare that old fellows like Low were very naughty boys indeed.

Well, I may not, and shall not, tell all the funny things that I have heard about the old doctor; but one story at least may be told, and no one need blush at its recital. Christmas and New Year were drawing near, and all the parish was bent on enjoyment. But there was one exception. In that turf-built cottage an old mini is sitting on his so-called easy-chair; the little shell lamp that burns beside him helps the December day to look longer than it really is; and the bright peat fire sheds a ruddy glow (that would have charmed the eye of a Rembrandt,) over the old doctor's face, as my father and I, after a quiet knock upon the door, lift the latch and 'step ben' as the cheery welcome strikes our ears.

With kindly tact the truth is elicited that funds had never been at so low an ebb before; the Yule and New Year that promised so much pleasure to almost all, had no welcome tidings for poor, poverty stricken Low; and as he dwelt fondly upon the rude yet hearty experiences of merrymakings now long gone by, and in which he himself played no unimportant part, a slight quaver came softly from his lips, and one big tear of regret rolled down his wrinkled cheek. The kindly visitor, however, had not come there that evening to add to the old man's sorrows, but to take some of them away if possible, and in a quiet and sympathetic way it was suggested that the doctor's gold watch should be shot for on Old Christmas Day by the sporting youths of Sillerton.

The passing of the watch into other hands would have

occasioned its present possessor no inconvenience whatever. It was now many years since the old timekeeper had in fact struck work. Its owner firmly believed that the motion connected with exercise on horseback was necessary to bring out all its sterling qualities, and that its silence now was caused simply because its wearer no longer patronized the gallop, but had descended to the more sober pace of 'Shank's mare.' Be that, however, as it may, it was then and there agreed to, that the gold watch should be shot for at Mains of Pitfuffie on old Christmas day; that subscription lists should be at once opened; and that the successful shot should wear the gold watch. Qui meruit palmam ferat, was the motto of our Sillerton Wapinschaw. Steadily went on the canvass during the days that intervened between that December evening and the day of the great shooting match.

There was no limit to the number of subscribers; the ancient timepiece possessed a value that half-crowns scarcely indicated; and when the youth of Sillerton stood to their guns on the heights of Pitfuffie on that bleak January morning (remember it was old style that we kept then) it was found that the old watch had realized for its owner nearly forty pounds sterling, no small sum among that quiet and simple people, and a perfect godsend to the impecunious old man. The cash had nil been deposited in the hands of the umpire, the rules and regulations had been duly read, and the firing briskly began. Old Christmas was certainly a legal holiday in Sillerton, though there were neither bank clerks nor Government officials there to enjoy their privileges, and it devolved upon the schoolboys alone, with a few dozen plowmen and hobbledehoys of the parish, to demonstrate that this was a day to be devoted fully and freely to social liberty and enjoyment.

Steadily from morn to night the guns blazed away, and the roll of subscribing marksmen was not completed until the shades of evening began to creep across the scarred brows of

Bennachie. No shot had gained a bull's eye, though there were a score at least of ties that had almost grazed the black ball that marked the center. These ties were about to be shot off, when the remark was made that my father, who had collected nearly nine-tenths, of the whole amount, and who was as well a liberal subscriber, was not on the ground, and had not claimed a shot.

It was then and there carried by acclamation that a shot should be fired on his behalf, his proxy being the exciseman, who was unquestionably the best shot in the parish. It was agreed, at the same time, that the ties should be fired off after the ganger's shot. A few moments of intense suspense came; the exciseman during that time looked as if carved out of Millstonehill granite; a puff of blue smoke at last came from the old musket, while every breath was hushed, and every eye strained to catch a glimpse of the now battered target. The marker quietly and deliberately performed his duty, and then leisurely faced the expectant crowd. At last the signal came a bull's eye! One shout rose over the field; no ties had to be shot off- the watch, the gold watch of the old doctor, had been waged and won, and in less time than it takes to tell it, I was hurrying homeward with that gold watch nestling in my breast pocket, while the temporary custodian of the same felt as proud and happy as if he had won and worn the Victoria Cross.

What were the thoughts that passed through my mind as I sped homewards that evening, I can scarcely tell. Probably I thought that as my father required but one watch, I was likely to become the happy owner of the gold one, but if not of that coveted prize, yet I felt that one of the watches must fall to my lot, assuredly under any circumstances. No sooner had my father arrived than I hastened to exhibit to him the trophy that he had won. He assured me that there was some mistake, as he had claimed no shot. I then recounted the occurrences of the day, and the firing of the shot that made the bull's eye. I shall never forget the look of sadness that stole over his features as I told my story. Probably he felt in his own mind that I was too young to take it upon myself to refuse the prize, but I know I felt supremely happy at that moment that I had expressed no craving for the ownership of the doctor's watch, and I believe he never once suspected the nature of my feelings.

"Go," said he, "at once to Dr. Low; give him again his watch with my compliments and say that I hope he may be long spared to wear it." Then in a low voice he added "I would not that that old man should fall asleep this night without his watch, no, not for all the gold watches that were ever made."

As I placed the prize half an hour later in the old doctor's hand, with my father's compliments and wishes, I heard no word of thanks spoken, but a silent tear stole down the furrowed cheek. I had seen a tear there once before; a tear of regret as he looked backward to a prosperous and merry past that could never return, arid as he felt and feared that only a gloomy future was in store for him. The tear that came now was the handmaid of a grateful heart, and whispered a message of deepest thanks that no language could have expressed so well. I returned home glad that I no longer wore a watch. Did my father feel that night, that it was more blessed to give than to receive?

CHAPTER X

HOW MARY MITCHELSON DISHED HER HUSBAND'S BROSE

"She has an ee, she has butane,
The cat has twa the very color,
Sic a wife as Willie had!"

Tall, wall-sided, speaking a dialect neither Scotch nor English, but made up of both, and wearing a green patch over one eye such was the subject of this sketch. This rude outline might have been drawn a year or two before old Dobbin became an orphan, and while John Forres, a young teacher from a peculiarly quiet and secluded parish of Aberdeenshire, was assistant to the old schoolmaster. I shall have occasion to touch lightly upon the young dominie by and by. Mary Mitchelson I called her, but probably I should have designated her Mrs. George Brodie. It was the custom, however, in Sillerton, and probably elsewhere, for some married ladies to retain their maiden names, just as ladies, in these modern days, celebrated in literature or art, or by rank or riches, often retain the name under which they won their spurs, if I may be allowed to use the expression with reference to the fair sex. It seems to me indeed that this was n\ore commonly the usage, perhaps I should have said universally the usage, when the gray mare was the better horse.

Well, Mary Mitchelson was a woman of pronounced character, and affected a style of language and genteel manners that seemed considerably above her social position as a Sillertonian. Poor, simple, homely Geordie Brodie was only a sawyer, and before saw-mills were common in Sillerton earned his living by converting the Scotch firs that covered nine-tenths of the parish into boards and scantling. The labors of a sawyer were necessarily severe, and as long distances had frequently to be traversed between the home of the laborer and his workshop, it was no wonder that Geovdie Brodie often returned home weary, ay, weary and hungry as well. This was just as it should be under ordinary circumstances; and when there was the wherewithal to satisfy the cravings of hunger, the fact itself should have suggested a feeling of gratitude, for our national bard puts it thus:

> "Some hae meat and canna eat.
> And some wad eat that want it;
> But we hae meat and we can eat,
> Andsae the Lord be thankit."

I have said that the sawyer should have been grateful for the feeling of. hunger under ordinary circumstances, but there was something more than ordinary in this case. Geordie Brodie and Mary Mitchelson were not precisely at one with regard to the quantity of, eatables that should satisfy the gnawing appetite of a healthy, hungry man. Mary, in fact, must have been first cousin to Mrs. Squeers, of Do-the-boys Hall, though she did not adopt the same tactics in turning the edge of the appetite. And so it happened that the sawyer frequently, nay, invariably, complained, of receiving short commons on his nightly return from his arduous labors. Philosophers had long ago discovered that. 'Nature abhorred a vacuum,' but it needed no philosopher to discover that when a vacuum existed in a man's stomach, the owner of said stomach was ill at ease with himself and the world. at large. Mary ignored this fact, and day after day, and week after week, continued to dole out to Geordie a measure of brose to his supper that lacked at least a third of the quantity that he considered should fall to his lot. Complaints, grumblings, and recriminations in consequence passed between the pair, until one evening matters came to a climax, and Geordie Brodie absolutely refused to even taste his usual allowance. Mary, instead of yielding that obedience that she had doubtless once promised, bitterly resented her husband's 'evil temper,' as she was pleased to call it, and brooded in silence over her own fancied wrongs. During the following day the same feeling absorbed her thoughts, until near the time when preparation had to be made for Geordie's return. Suddenly a happy thought seemed to strike Mrs. Brodie, and a smile of satisfaction flitted across her saturnine, pinched features. Eureka (I have found it), Mary might have exclaimed, had she known Greek, but, Greek or no Greek, she had found a happy solution to the problem that she had been so long pondering in her mind. To think, with Mary, was to act. She at once rose from her seat beside the fire that she had been stirring in anticipation of preparing her husband's evening meal, and hastened to the byre, that was only a few dozen of yards from the house. There, providing herself with the wooden trough in which the cow was usually supplied with her allowance of boiled turnips and chaff, Mary was soon again in her own kitchen. The trough was duly placed on the table where Geordie Brodie's cap of brose usually stood; a large quantity of oatmeal, butter, and boiling water were stirred together in the lordly dish, and with a grim smile of satisfaction, Mary awaited the denouement.

She had not long to wait. Brodie almost immediately entered the little apartment that served the double purpose of kitchen and dining room, and hungry and tired, as usual, his eye naturally turned to the table. A sarcastic jibe from his better-half might have accelerated his scrutinizing glance. Be that, however, as it may, the hungry sawyer took in the whole situation at once. And then, what a storm arose! Little did the wife anticipate the furious rage that, in one moment, converted the quiet and douce Geordie Brodie into a raving maniac. But so it was.

What then and there took place was never known.

Geordie Brodie went next morning to his daily toil as usual. Young Geordie for they had one son looked after such matters as required some attention outside, and only after a long month's seclusion did Mary Mitchelson appear in the Sillerton Square. But an altered woman was she. Her stiff and unshapely form seemed even more acute-angled than before; the sarcastic smile was perceptibly intensified, and to crown all there was a green patch over one of her eyes, that was never removed during the many years that she thereafter lived in Sillerton. Poor Mary had few friends, and did little to conciliate the few who might have been friendly to her. Her bite was ever readier than her smile, and scathing sarcasm came more freely and naturally from her lips than commendation and praise. Sarcasm, indeed, with Mary Mitchelson was always upon a hair-trigger. Once more we venture to fill up a background. The son, Geordie junior, was a pupil in the parish school, at this time taught by the assistant of Louis Alexander. One day during the recital of the forenoon lessons, the door suddenly opened, the face of Mary Mitchelson appeared, and a shrill and somewhat angry voice demanded "George! where did you put the jocktaleg before you went to school?" The question was put in words that stood out singly, as it were, and which were scarcely in the style commonly used in Sillerton. Very different were the accent and tone that came from Geordie, "In the greep ahint the coo, mither." The effect was irresistible.

Even the smallest Scotch heads took it in. One roar of laughter rose from all present, which was also participated in by the youthful assistant. Mary, however, quailed not under the ridicule that her visit and question had evoked, but, ignoring all the others, she fixed her one eye upon the poor but guilty dominie, and speaking slowly, as if desiring that every word she uttered should be a species of dagger-thrust, she annihilated him with the scathing remark:

"What could you expect out of Leochel?" Leochel, I may explain, was the native parish of the teacher. The door banged loudly and Mary Mitckelson was gone.

Her remark, however, remained behind, and became a byword in the parish of Sillerton, and I doubt not, were I fortunate enough to ever revisit those scenes of my boyhood, I should still hear, many a time, a free and Scotch translation of the Jewish proverb, "Can any good thing come out of Nazareth"

CHAPTER XI

THE QUEEN'S SCOTCH AS SPOKEN IN SILLERTON

"But he, I ween, was of the north countrie."

Beattie's "Minstrel".

It was stated in the foregoing chapter that Mary Mitchelson spoke a dialect somewhat different from that used in Sillerton. At the same time it may be explained, that, for causes to be given, the Scotch of the Sillertonians was not precisely identical with that spoken in other parishes of the Garioch, and especially in places lying to the west and north of the parish. It is curious sometimes to note the effects produced even by a range of hills surrounding a small community, and shutting it out, so to speak, from other communities; effects that influence, in no small degree, language, character, both mental and physical, and last, but not least, religion itself. I recollect well, in boyhood's days, when spending my holiday among the hills that lie between the Don and Spey, I more than once came upon a community of Roman Catholics living snugly in some sheltered valley that had remained uninfluenced by the great Reformation that had swept over Scotland, but which had passed them by, simply on account of the gigantic bulwark of rocks and hills that rendered communication with the people living within this barrier very difficult, if not well-nigh impossible.

I remember meeting on the Gaudie side of Bennachie, two members of the Royal Academy of Painters, one of whom, the celebrated so-called 'Philip of Spain,' was searching closely for types of genuine Scottish faces, with which to fill up a historical scene he was painting. I sent him to such a spot as I have just described, the Cabrach, and years afterwards he assured me that he had found there exactly what he wanted. As to the influence of such a locality on language there can be no doubt whatever, and hence the Grampian range, that sheltered Sillerton from the west and north, rendered Sillerton's speech somewhat different from that spoken beyond the dividing line. There were other causes as well to influence our speech. Sillerton was, in one respect, somewhat ambitious, and among the farmers who cultivated its fair meadows and sunny slopes there were several who had enjoyed the privilege of a college education. I do not mean to say that these men had given themselves the trouble of working for a degree in Arts, but four years at the University had made them at least fair scholars, while four years' intercourse with youths drawn from all parts of Scotland served, in no small measure, to influence their Doric Scotch, and through them to influence others with whom they were daily associated.

The degrees were more in the way of professional men; and ministers, schoolmasters, and medicals (we seemed to educate no lawyers in Sillerton) deemed it at least advisable to go in for the degree of M. A.

From this it is evident that the Queen's Scotch was somewhat different among the upper ten of Sillerton society, for we were strictly conservative in those days, and when invited to a dance, dinner, or picnic, could always tell precisely who the individuals were, they at least of the parish, who would receive and accept invitations. All this had its influence beyond the immediate circle, like the stone cast into a still pond, that not only makes a splurge in the very spot where it falls, but sends countless ripples away on every side to the very shore. In fact, one can scarcely conceive how easily and readily language is affected by the circumstances that surround us, and I remember well the remark of a pawky farmer of Sillerton in corroboration of this assertion on our part. A neighbor remarked that his 'orra' man spoke in a style quite different from that used by the other servants. "Oh, aye," said the carl, "I mice sent Jock on some business to the Lothians; he was awa a hale fortnicht, and he has spoken pure English ever Since syne."

There was also another factor at work which in due course affected the Queen's Scotch as spoken in Sillerton. Not many years before the commencement of my school-days, a good deal of Scotch was spoken by our schoolmasters, and it was no uncommon circumstance to hear a commentary on a chapter of the Bible conducted from the pulpit in genuine Scotch. This was not the case with the Rev. Robert Fordyce, for with him both bearing and language were dignity personified, but slightly farther north the old Scotch still held its sway, and an esteemed class-fellow of mine told me that he heard a noted divine, not many miles from Aberlour, use the following 'grace before supper' on one occasion "For what I and the ither three lads are aboot to receive, Lord, rnak' us a' truly thankfu'. Amen."

In this case, however, we must bear in mind that there was no doubt whatever about what language the speaker intended to use, and the Rev. Mr. Wilson, of Aberlour, spoke Scotch because he liked to speak it, and because probably he found himself more at home in it than were he using the Queen's English. But in the case of educated men who knew English well, who could spell it correctly, and, were perfectly conversant with its grammar and idioms, we are well aware that they were frequently not acquainted with the proper vowel sounds. This fact is pointed out in the life of the author of 'Tullochgorum.' In one of Skinner's pieces, which is written in the purest English, the rhyme shows this defect. The piece we refer to is 'John of Badenyon,' and it is at least interesting to note how frequently the long sound of 'o' is made to rhyme to the last syllable of the name of the hero, which is unquestionably short. Of course it might be pleaded that there are certain 'allowable rhymes,' and that the greatest English poets have availed themselves of the privilege when necessary. In Pope we find the following lines:

"Thus Pegasus, a nearer way to take,
May boldly deviate from the common track"

And in Dryden we have the following:

"The sun his annual course obliquely made,
Good days contracted and enlarg'd the bad."

We might indeed quote such examples by the hundred. This was undoubtedly a species of poetical license, but among my own personal clerical friends there were a half-dozen at least, who, in certain vowel sounds, and especially when in the pulpit, used liberties with the Queen's English positively startling, and it always appeared a puzzle to me how such pronunciation could have been acquired. But such it was.

Doubtless, the introduction of railways, and a freer intercourse between the natives on both sides of the Tweed have done much during the last half century to enable even the more highly-educated Scot to distinguish correctly between the different sounds of the same vowel, and we doubt not, that the next northern bard who tries his hand at a new version of 'John o' Badenyon' will steer clear, without difficulty, of those solecisms that were erewhile committed by the genial pastor of Linshart. I knew intimately a very excellent divine on Donside; a man distinguished for his learning; valued and honored in Church courts; eloquent either on the platform or in the pulpit; and above all one of the most genial of men, and yet as to his pronunciation of the Queen's English he was a veritable barbarian. The witty editor of an Aberdeen weekly remarked, that it was a pity that the learned and popular minister of T had, in his youth, got a spurious edition of Walker's pronouncing dictionary.

But, after all, are these things to be considered strange in the case of Scotchmen, when we find Englishmen themselves sometimes, nay oftentimes, anything but correct in the pronunciation of their own language? I have heard in an English Cathedral from the lips of a graduate of an English University, and from one, too, enjoying those marks of distinction after his name that stamp men eminent for scholarship I have heard, I say, false pronunciation of English that was perfectly startling. Need we wonder then when we hear an educated Scotchman calling a Presbyterian Synod 'this reverend coort,' or employing equally eccentric modes of speech that should have been eliminated, if not in the nursery, then in the parish school? I may remark here, that the inspectorship of schools also, in connection with bequests that applied to our parochial system, made it imperative that a sound English education should be given in our schools, and while the classics and mathematics scarcely jarred with the pure Doric of the Garioch, yet with the teaching of English it was quite different. It was indeed difficult to find teachers in those days who had anything like a correct idea of the different vowel sounds, and how could they, under the circumstances?

Many of our teachers held that English grammar was unnecessary where the Latin grammar had to be taught, and hence, while spelling and some other things were correct enough, yet the pronunciation was sadly defective. Here, however, is a case in point. The inspector of the Dick Bequest was examining a school not far from the shady side of Bennachie, and took occasion to correct a class for their inattention to the different sounds of the vowel 'u,' the word 'bull' having occurred in the lesson, and pointing out in the dictionary key, how the vowel should be sounded in different words. The dominie could not stand this, but interrupted the proceedings with the remark, 'Na, n a, sir; it's bull, full, pull,' pronouncing the three words in the broadest Doric, Scotch, 'an' the loons are richt.'

This may be an exceptional case, but doubtless its existence in a greater or less extent brought it about, that when a vacancy occurred in Sillerton, the place was filled by young men who had enjoyed a town training in addition to the usual classical education. This was truly the piece of leaven that leavened the lump. Old Louis Alexander Daff indoctrinated his pupils with as pure Latinity as we got from the more modern teachers, but the latter taught us English Grammar, and gave us such a pronunciation of English as would enable us to become tutors in any of our more ambitious Scotch families, or even successful teachers beyond the border in English schools. Gentle reader, bear in mind that it is not here pretended that the youths of Sillerton succeeded in acquiring an English accent. No, no; not often do we find Scotchmen who do this, and while we occasionally meet our countrymen who were perhaps educated in England, and who had been long strangers to the land of the heather, speaking a language that would scarcely indicate their nationality, yet when we enter into familiar conversation with them, there generally slips out a word or phrase that betrays its northern origin. It is not universally the case that the accent remains, but it is very frequently so, and in proof I may mention an incident that happened in my own experience. Dining at a mess table, where I had the honor of performing the duties of regimental chaplain, an English lady who sat next to me said, "How is it that Scotchmen so often retain their Scotch accent, even after many years' absence from Scotland? I have often asked the question, but I confess that I have never received a satisfactory answer." I replied that I felt satisfied that it would be unnecessary for her to ask the same question again, as I could give a conclusive answer. "How is it then?" she inquired. Raising my head, and looking as dignified as possible. I replied, "We are proud of our accent."

"Ah! I just thought as much." There was a slight lull in the conversation, and I very quietly threw in the additional information, "But, madam, there is another reason, for were we to try to get rid of our accent I do believe that we would find it impossible." It is needless to say that I brought down the house and that my fair questioner laughingly remarked, "I am quite satisfied now."

I shall close this chapter with showing the care that our pedagogues took not only in teaching what they held to be pure English, but in getting their pupils to read with an eye to punctuation as well, without which the sense of the passage might have escaped them altogether. A neighboring teacher fell upon the unique plan of getting his pupils to pronounce the word 'tick' whenever a comma occurred in a sentence; a semi-colon and colon received two 'ticks,' while the full stop elicited three 'ticks.' This was to be practiced, however, for a short time only, and as the school examination approached, the 'ticks' were duly dropped, and 'dummy ticks,' so to speak, were used instead.

The great day at last came, and the Bible-class was paraded for duty. Unfortunately the dux had been absent for a few days, and had not been made aware of the new order for abolishing the 'ticks.' The chapter for the day was duly pointed out, and the dux, evidently in his nervousness, skipping several important parts of the passage, yet, in a clear and distinct voice, astonished the listening divines with a new rendering of the Scripture lesson: "And the Lord said unto Moses, tick, say unto the children of Israel, tick, tick; and Moses said unto the children of Israel, tick, tick, tick."

And lastly, as some of our preachers were wont to say, even after the conclusion, I shall instance the case of Willie Nuckel, so called, a crofter in the village, who nearly lost his croft by inattention to the due punctuation of his speech, if I may so designate the blunder. Nuckel evidently had never been duly drilled in school days in the proper use of the 'ticks,' and in consequence nearly came to grief. Nuckel was the owner of a horse called Diamond, why so called I am now unable to say probably for some excellent qualities that the animal possessed. In those days few pedestrians were allowed to pass through the Home Park, which separated the laird's residence from the village of Sillerton, and to be seen there with a horse and cart, or in fact with any vehicle whatever, would have been considered a species of sacrilege.

Nuckel, however, had received orders from the proper quarter, and early one morning was met by the laird while carting a load of fallen branches from the said park to the village. The somewhat irate proprietor demanded of Nuckel, and not in very pleasant tones, why and what he was carting there. Nuckel was decidedly in a hurry, and was little inclined to parley with any one, the only words heard by the squire being, "Sticks for the forester ye brute Diamond, get up."

Poor Nuckel was served with the usual notice to leave his croft and cottage at next Martinmas, the laird having imagined that the word 'brute' was applied to himself personally. A due explanation stayed the sentence, and Nuckel sleeps in Sillerton churchyard. The obnoxious epithet, after all, was really not intended for the laird, but for the horse; but still the proper application of the 'tick' in the right place, would have in this case saved days and weeks, nay, months, of misery.

CHAPTER XII

JEAN BARDEN'S MILK FOE BABES

"Though the 'Brownie o' Blednoch' lang be gane,
The mark o' his feet's left on mony a stane;
An' mony a wife an' mony a wean
Tell the feats of Aiken-drum.
E'en now, light loons that jibe an' sneer
At spiritual guests an' a' sic gear,
At the Glashnoch mill hae swat wi' fear,
An' looked roun' for Aiken-drum.
And guidly folks hae gotten a fright,
When the moon was set, and the stars gied nae light,
At the roaring linn in the howe o' the night,
Wi' sughs like Aiken-drum."

The Brownie o' Blednoch.

I often wonder if those who were most zealous in indoctrinating our young minds with all the superstitions of those days ever reflected on the great wrong they were doing. I wonder if they ever thought that it would take, in some cases, the effort of years to root out the weeds that they were then so anxious to sow; nay, that in some cases so deeply would these weeds penetrate into the mind, that they would grow with our growth, and blossom as freely in old age, as when we clung to our mother's apron strings.

It is said that noted travelers who have spent years among savage tribes, even when they return to civilization, dread to hear a footstep behind them, and peer cautiously into a room before they enter it. And men I have personally known, who had borne themselves bravely through many a hard-fought and bloody field, yet when the shadows of night came down, would not have gone alone a hundred yards in the dark, no matter what the bribe might be that sought to tempt them. And all this, at least in the latter case, very probably originated in the habit, doubtless long established, of telling stories of a blood-curdling character to the young. Jean Burden was pre-eminently the story teller of Sillerton. It was true that the meal-miller could spin a wonderful yarn about water-kelpies and their strange doings, and how the miller word, when properly and artistically handled, could instantaneously arrest a water-wheel in full career and perform sundry other wonderful things all of which tales were greedily swallowed by many of the miller's audience, for audience he often had when the first oats of the season began to arrive at Damhead. But the burly miller could not hold a candle to Jean, who, both in yield and variety, distanced every competitor.

The fact is, that at this distant date, it would be difficult to specify exactly the points possessed by Jean that enabled her to outstrip all other rivals. It is possible that one point was the variety of beings of supernatural origin that filled her repertoire. The miller had only two strings to his bow the miller word and the water-kelpie; the blacksmith, during the intervals that occurred between the hammering of the iron and the reheating of it again, dealt chiefly with feats of manly strength that he had witnessed; while the tailor and his apprentice, who made periodical visits to Sillerton to re-clothe the males of the village-in new garments, retailed pretty much the gossip that they gathered during their wanderings throughout the country, and which, in those quiet times, when 'dailies' were yet undreamed of, were alike interesting to high and low, and young and old. I had almost forgotten little Sandy Simms, the cobbler, but I am now under the impression that his forte lay in relating stories that very graphically brought out the pawky character of Scottish humor. But Jean operated in another field altogether the horrible in what was human, and the blood-curdling in what was supernatural, being the commodities in which she dealt. Nor was her stock of these by any means limited, as kelpies, goblins, fairies, brownies, elves, ghosts, wizards, witches, and sundry others of a kindred nature, were to her household words. Had she been requested to describe these, I doubt not Jean would have done so with ease, and classified them to the entire satisfaction of the most exacting scientist. Then, in addition to melancholy songs and ballads, all invariably of a lugubrious character, and covering a wide field of weird literature, her vivid imagination, and her peculiar faculty of finding suitable words to express her meaning, would alone have made her remarkable in any community. To us she certainly was remarkable, and charmed us as the snake charms its unresisting prey.

Jean, along with her husband and family, occupied a small cottage in the village square of Sillerton. Her husband, the only Seceder, we believe, in the parish, we mean apart from a few members of the Episcopal Church, was wont on winter evenings to wend his way after supper to the house of a neighbor, where politics and religion were freely discussed. Jean was thus pretty much left to her own devices during the evening, and she employed her time thoroughly. I see that kitchen now, just as I used to see it fifty years ago. There is only an earthen floor, and apart from the dim light that is supplied by half a dozen smoldering peats, the only attempt at lighting the humble apartment is by a splinter of fir root stuck in a link of the crook or chain that hangs in the chimney, and as one of these primitive candles is consumed, another is lighted and put in its place.

As if by concert, at a certain hour every evening, the youngsters of the village congregate in Jean's kitchen. The few stools and benches, or deeces, more properly called, that were distributed round the kitchen are soon filled by the expectant crowd. But I had almost forgotten the seat of honor on these occasions. This was at the two opposite sides of the capacious chimney which stretched half across the gable of the house, and where three or four urchins could easily find both snug and ample quarters. These seats were, however, difficult to obtain, and were for two reasons much sought after by the audience. The first reason was, that on a cold winter night, there was a warmth there not to be found in any other part of the house, and the second was (we will own a somewhat peculiar one) that the occupants of these seats could not be attacked from the rear, and no matter what happened, they were comparatively safe in that quarter. Jean Burden sits on, or rather in, one of these huge wooden four-poster chairs that have become fashionable again, but now wearing brighter colors than their more homely prototype. Without any preliminary remarks whatever, Jean commences her tale of the evening, and with little or no interruption, except from a renewal of a light that had burned out, or on account of a chip of fir that had accidentally fallen down, the tale goes on for at least an hour and a half.

At this distant date, I could not restore, so to speak, one story that Jean ever told, but there are certainly pieces of many of them that still cling tenaciously to the memory. Just read over the horrors that Tain O'Shanter saw in Alloa Kirk, and you will have a fair idea of the species of literature on which we feasted on those wintry nights. One evening we had a ghost story in all its weird associations; a ghost that came and went like a gleam of light; some unquiet spirit perhaps that left the earth with some momentous secret upon its soul, and that was permitted to revisit scenes with which it was once familiar in the flesh, in order to communicate what it knew to some one bold enough to demand its errand. At another time we had stories connected with troublesome times when fire and sword swept even the peaceful Garioch; while occurrences of the '45' were reproduced, but all tinged with those shades of coloring that Jean's skillful hand knew so well how to apply.

Then, again, we had the account of some dreadful murder that had once been committed within the bounds. The circumstances are all laid before us; the culprit is described and produced in Court; the trial takes place once more; the prisoner is found guilty; the judge puts on the terrible black cap of doom; the ghastly gallows appears, and the tragedy ends with probably a few verses of a melancholy song that the unhappy man is supposed to have composed on the very morning of his execution, something, in fact, finding a counterpart in the Banff freebooter who:

"Played a tune and danced it roun'
Beneath the gallows-tree."

As to robberies, they were numerous 'as leaves in Vallombrosa,' and had comparatively little interest unless someone was shot or knifed on the occasion. In fact, things of the ordinary class had no charms for us. Of dismal love-stories also there were not a few, and in all these cases the course never did run smooth. Stern fathers and unfeeling mothers arose to forbid the banns; there were insuperable difficulties that could not begot over, and in consequence, we bad a whole school of 'Mill o' Tiftie's Annies,' and too frequently the conclusion poured forth the melancholy wail

"My true love died for me to-day;
I'll die for him to-morrow."

In fact Jean's chamber of horrors would not have yielded to that of Madame Tussaud, and was different only in this, that the wax figure appealed simply to the eye, and was dumb, while Jean's brilliant imagination not only placed the individuals before the mental eye, but made each one tell his own tale. Truly the dry bones that Jean Barden laid before us did not long remain such. There was soon a shaking among them, and under her magic touch, they became clothed anew with all the outward appearances of animated life, and speedily found living tongues to record once more their own experiences.

There was also one peculiarity about many of Jean's ghost stories that gave them an interest that we could not otherwise have so keenly felt; they were localized and connected with places that we all knew well. In fact, there were few lonely places in the parish without some brownie, or fairy, or boodie of evil odor associated with it, and there we sat and shivered, and listened with rapt attention while the story sped on its way; listened with mouths and eyes widely opened to drink in all the absorbing details; listened with a growing terror in our hearts at what might be, for all we knew, very near ourselves. And when the last word was spoken, and Jean, rising from her lecture chair, waved us to the door with the somewhat abrupt good night; "Noo, bairns, siff to bed," we scampered off like a flock of frightened sheep.

None of us had very far to go, but short as was the distance that intervened between Jean Burden's kitchen and my father's house, I would rather have run the gauntlet between two lines of Indian braves, than traverse the few yards that I had to cover till I reached my own door. I fancied that there was a perfect host of malignant spirits behind me, with no running stream to bar pursuit. And so it happened, that as the paternal door closed behind me, I felt, only then, that I could breathe again in safety. The question, indeed, might be asked, "But why listen to stories that produced such disagreeable consequences; why go when the returning was accompanied by such terrors as might have well kept us at home?" Alas! gentle reader, is it then hard to find an answer? Look at that poor bewildered moth circling nearer and nearer the flame that at last consumes its beauteous wings, and leaves it scorched and helpless on the ground to die. And has it never happened in your own experience, that you have felt just like that scorched moth not while you were circling round your alluring light, but when wings and hope all gone you felt scorched and helpless?

We may not press the question further, for we well know what the answer should be, were the truth the simple truth the whole truth told. And so with us poor youngsters. There was a glamour about Jean Barden and her stories that we could not resist, and night after night, and week after week did we listen, until they became part and parcel of ourselves. And what was the consequence? There was not a youth among us that would have gone through the Home Park, or the Howe o' Coghard, after nightfall, could he by so doing have earned his weight in gold. Had we told at home all that we had heard, it might have been very different, but we evidently kept all this to ourselves. At the same time, in those days, there was little censorship exercised over tales told in the kitchen, and very probably there would have been no alarm at the result, even had the whole been known.

I shall now step into the witness-box, and to show the unwholesomeness of such milk as Jean ladled out to the youngsters of Sillerton, I shall honestly relate what I experienced on the very first trip that I made, after nightfall, and alone. I had been promised a pair of 'Bantams,' by a farmer living somewhere beyond Pitcaple that is to say, about fifteen miles from Sillerton. On a bright summer morning during the harvest holidays I saddled my pony, strapped on my back a suitable basket, and started for the home of my Bantams, the name of which place I have forgotten. I reached the farm all right, but every one was engaged in harvest work in the distant fields, and so it happened that before I got my Bantams in my basket, and I was duly mounted on Donald's back, the sun had gone clown and dark shadows were stealing along the sides and slopes of Bennachie.

There was not much very startling in this, but as I trotted on, the shadows grew darker, until I found that I had to find my way home over a good dozen Scotch miles, and in the dark. This was my first experience of such a trial, and I certainly felt it. When I arrived at Gaudy Ford, the river seemed to me to have risen since I passed during the day, and there was a noise of rushing waters that kept me pondering on the bank for some time. At last, however, realizing the fact that home lay beyond the ford, and recollecting that Donald could swim well, and so could his master, I pushed on and through, and found that the stillness of night and the deep gloom had both combined to make things look worse than they actually were. Gaudy crossed and left behind, new troubles and fresh horrors came. The road passed along the base of Bennachie, and in many places, as I came nearer Sillerton, I mean the boundaries of the parish, it was approached on both sides by deep woods that sometimes completely overshadowed it. Then there were unearthly, uncanny sounds that fell harshly upon the ear; the roe deer would occasionally make a startled run from approaching footsteps, and the short yap of the disturbed fox, as he scurried across the road, had a most depressing effect upon my spirits. Courage I had almost said, but no; all the courage I once had had oozed out. It required a supreme effort of the will to enable me to make any progress whatever, even under the most ordinary circumstances, and when more than ordinary dangers seemed near well, then, a shake of the basket which started a cackle of the fowls huddled within it, and a quiet but fervent repetition of the Lord's Prayer, gave me renewed strength and backbone, and I trotted on. The Howe o' Coghard was my last painful experience on that eventful journey. Jean Barden had shown a special favor for this place, and brownies, witches, and warlocks ghosts with heads and without them were there sighs and sounds that seemed to come from another world were often heard there, and in fact a finer field for awe-inspiring, gruesome influences could scarcely be imagined. I felt all this keenly. The horrible stories associated with the place all rushed back upon a memory that was perhaps on this occasion too retentive, and cautiously I drew bridle before plunging into the dismal shades of Coghard. The evening was now far spent. My progress had been unusually slow, as I had literally to often feel my way, and over and above the darkness of an autumn moonless night, there was an unpleasant sough among the tree-tops that threatened rain. There was, however, no help for it. I would have sooner joined a forlorn hope, and stormed a deadly breach, than ride that night through the Howe o'Coghard, but yet my home in Sillerton was beyond. How that basket rattled on my back, how the Bantams cackled and protested, and how fervently my prayers were said, I cannot tell now, but with the encouragement derived from both, and a more than usually liberal use of the heel upon Donald, the Howe was speedily and safely passed, and I soon thereafter found myself in the village of Sillerton. The same sensations I never again experienced. I was during that solitary ride almost cured of my superstitious weaknesses; Jean Barden's teachings were, by a supreme, perhaps heroic effort, ignominiously cast aside, and I then learned to laugh at terrors, that have ere now turned some black heads almost instantaneously white. Jean, we doubt not, was honest in her convictions, as far as they went, and plied her art to the end of life, and doubtless was often thanked for the amusement she afforded the youngsters. I must say, however, for myself, that had I learned that any one had been indoctrinating my own young barbarians with such poison as I had personally sucked in Jean Barden's fir-lighted kitchen in the village of Sillerton fifty years ago, I would have said with the genial author of the "Ewie wi' the Crookit Horn":

"O! gin I had the loun that did it,
Sworn I hae, as well as said it,
Tho' a' the warld should forbid it,
I wad gie his neck a thraw."

CHAPTER XIII

THE POOR PRIOR TO THE POOR LAWS

"For ye have the poor with you always."

St. Mark XIV 7

Before Poor Laws were enacted, there existed a very primitive state of things as to those who were denominated the poor. I do not mean to say that there were really no paupers, but poverty, at least in country places, did not appear very oppressive. Most people put forth an effort to aid in supporting their poor relations; the Kirk-Session sent, per the hands of the elders, a quarterly dole of a few shillings to gladden the hearts of the aged recipients, occasionally there were charities that provided a pittance for the deserving poor, and almost always, there were milk and meal, and perhaps a few things besides, that found their way from the farmhouse to the humble abodes of those who, in some respects, like the Russian serf, seemed to belong to the soil. It should be mentioned, also, that one or two channels there were, in addition to the means already stated, by which the old and indigent could eke out their somewhat contracted living, so that altogether the inevitably poor could manage to get the two ends to meet.

This chapter is headed "The Poor prior to the Poor Laws." This heading is selected advisedly, since my acquaintance with the poor, under the new system, dated several years later in fact, after I had left college. That these laws were necessary there can be no doubt, but as little doubt is there, that, by their operation, a change for the worse was produced in the minds of the Scottish peasantry, and that honest pride, that stinted itself to keep a poor relative from becoming a charge on the parish, entirely died away, and, instead, the more matter of fact feeling crept in "If I pay my public rates, then my private charity ceases."

With this brief explanation of the reason why I circumscribe my acquaintance with those requiring charity, I shall at once proceed with the subject more immediately before me, and show how much or how little I knew of the poor of Sillerton, before the Poor Laws were enacted for their benefit. In close proximity to several of the large farms, there were one or two cottages occupied by aged people, who had, perhaps, in younger days, been employed as laborers on the farm. Did I say 'cottages?' Well, that would be a misnomer. These dwellings were huts of the most primitive character, built of rough stones and sods, compacted together somehow; thatched with straw or heather, and with a floor made of clay that had received much the same treatment it would have got in a brick-yard, with the exception of the baking process, which, in this case, was never applied, the feet of the occupants and the footsteps of time being deemed sufficient to render this primitive floor fit for the purpose it was intended to serve. There was generally but one bole, or small window, looking out to the south; two windows being in order when the dwelling boasted a 'but and a ben.'

There was no ceiling in these simple abodes, and the wood or peat fires that burned upon large slab-stones that formed the hearth produced a smoke that curled gracefully among the blackened rafters, until it found its way out by a hole in the roof, that could scarcely be called by the respectable name of a chimney, but which, at the same time, did duty for that excellent institution. I do not mean to insinuate in the slightest degree that these huts were not comfortable, and that their occupants were not quite contented with them; but they certainly had their drawbacks. In certain conditions of the weather the smoke seemed to get bewildered, and could not find its way to the usual place of exit, but then the occupants, like the traditional eels, were used to this pyroligneous tribulation, though I honestly confess that, to one unaccustomed to it, it would have been simply intolerable. An old friend in Canada, who had amassed a large fortune, told me that he had once taken a holiday to go and visit his aged mother, who lived near the banks of the Spey. He was most anxious to spend a few days with the old lady, but was literally driven out of the house by the smoke, and had to take up his quarters in the hotel at Carr-Bridge, whence he could make occasional trips to visit her.

Willingly would he have built a chimney, but the old woman demurred. That would have been an innovation that would have completely upset all her arrangements, and the son left his aged parent contented to live and die in the smoke. Speaking of smoke in Scotland reminds me of an incident that once happened in Canada to a couple of officers of the Royal Engineers and your humble servant, then officiating chaplain for that distinguished corps, and on which occasion smoke played a conspicuous part. We had gone, during the bleak and stormy month of January, to shoot, 'promiscuously,' I may call it, in that primeval forest of yellow pine that then mantled the banks of the Chaudiere, and in which there then existed a paradise both for the sportsman and for the lumberman.

We were the guests of a member of the latter class, and spent three or four days, I should rather say nights, in one of his camps, which was built in what was once the hunting-grounds of the Abenaki Indians, of whom only one family lived now in all that region. That we were comfortable generally goes without saying. The old cook had once worn Her Majesty's uniform, and his heart warmed when he found that his guests were of the militant profession, whether clerical or otherwise, and every effort was put forth to render us as comfortable as gastronomic art could make us. If pork and beans, the other luxuries that are to be found in a lumber camp, and the ordinary etceteras that we brought along with us, could make mortals happy, we had been happy indeed. But the Bubbly Jock was there, even in that primitive camp. The large 'caboose' that occupied the center of the shanty would persist in sending jets of smoke indiscriminately to every corner of the camp. Had it been summer, and had the mosquitoes and other pests that then hold high holiday in Canadian woods been in force, we might have submitted with a good grace to the smudge that was constantly and ruthlessly permeating our whole system. We held a council of war; our highest scientific skill was brought into play to devise a cure for the smoke nuisance, and after mature deliberation we felt that we could successfully grapple with and conquer our enemy.

So far, so well. Peter Farley, the cook, was invited to join our caucus. He was shown the method we proposed to employ, to get rid of the vile smoke that was gradually lessening the distance between us arid the noble red man, and we dreamed in imagination so fondly dreamed of a few hours of serene, unclouded happineess in that camp, and in our exuberance of joy we asked Farley if we had not completely solved the difficulty. Peter not for one moment hesitated. In his mind the smoke question had been long solved, and it gave him no trouble whatever to unfold his opinion on the matter. "Well, gentlemen," said the ex-private of Her Majesty's 16th Foot, and now chief cook of Grande Roche Camp, "we are not in England, and if you cure the smoke, there is no saying but that some of the boys may find fault with the cooking."

Having delivered himself of this oracular response, Farley left us to our own meditations, and quickly disappeared in the commingling cloud of smoke and steam that whirled and floated around and above the blazing caboose. It was very evident to us that there were other things that troubled more the anxious cook than the vile pyroligneous acid that might pinch the eyes or excite the choler of his sorrowful guests, who verily had been gradually developing into a species of human 'weeping willows.'

Our fate was undoubtedly sealed; from Peter's judgment there was no appeal. Another twenty four hours' rubbing in of this 'Indian tan' would make us as yellow as the moccasins that we wore, and we simply bent to the inevitable. The very rapid depletion of our cigar-cases within the next half-hour, and the dense volume of tobacco-smoke that rose above us and gradually joined issue with the mightier cloud into which Farley had incontinently disappeared, might have easily convinced the most skeptical unbeliever, that the guests of the genial proprietor of Grand Roche Camp were firm believers in the great maxim of the homceopathists Similia similibus curantur 'Likes are cured by likes.'

To return to our Sillerton poor and their smoky dwellings, we may remark, that, if they disregarded the smoke, they were equally callous with regard to the question of light. In fact, there came less light from the miniature window than from the peat fire that smoldered on the hearth. But yet the occupants were contented therewith; they did not really require much light; their duties inside were not of such a nature as to require the glare of an electric fifty-candle-power carbon-burner, and if additional light were necessary, it could readily be produced in a decidedly primitive way, namely, by sticking a lighted fir-spunk in a link of the crook that hung over the fireplace. In fact, they objected on principle to the enlargement of their windows.

On one occasion, along with my father, I visited an old man who lived somewhere near the old house of Tillyfour in such a hut as I have described. James Marnoch was then upwards of a hundred years of age, but still retained all his faculties, and was quite able to care in every way for himself. In James's hut there was no window whatever, and all the light of heaven he received, he did so on the outside of his biggin', or in a subdued form down the chimney. The Lady of Sillerton took much kindly interest in the poor of the parish, and provided many a little comfort for them that came in handy during the cold months of winter. Marnoch was one of her favorites, and generally received a visit from his benefactress occasionally during the summer.

Late in autumn she left for England, but before leaving, usually constituted my father her almoner, and to him entrusted whatever she had provided for her numerous pensioners, accompanied oftentimes with kindly messages, and hopeful wishes for their welfare. To Marnoch, on this occasion, were handed sundry parcels containing clothing, tea, sugar, and many small yet necessary articles besides. To deliver these was an easy matter, but I observed that my father had evidently something else to communicate, but apparently he had some difficulty in broaching it. At last, out it came. He had received instructions to get a window placed in the hut, as an improvement that his benefactress doubtless thought would be heartily appreciated by the centenarian. My father had doubts on that subject, and these were speedily confirmed. Marnoch expressed his grateful thanks for all the kindness received, but positively refused to accept the window. He had got accustomed to the light that came in by open door, or chimney, and more light would be disagreeable to him, and, in addition to this, the opening of a space for the proposed improvement might admit the cold as well as the light. James Marnoch lived and died in that hut, but no window was ever inserted in its wall.

One source of earning a few shillings now and then came to those poor creatures, at least to the women, in the way of knitting stockings and other clothing. There was always a demand for such articles among a class, that had neither the inclination nor perhaps the time to do such work, and where the small charge made was certainly a temptation to get the knitting done elsewhere than at home. But beyond the local trade, if I might so call it, there was a larger trade that found abundant employment for such as were able and willing to work. An agent for some manufacturing firm, or firms, made periodical visits to Sillerton, on which occasions he supplied his knitters with yarn, and at the same time received from them the articles finished since his former visit. It is true that very small prices were allowed for such work, but yet what they received was to them a sort of 'Godsend,' and, after all, the work required made but little demand upon their time, and, in fact, it often appeared to me that the old 'bodies' could go on with their knitting under any circumstances, and without any apparent effort whatever.

It is at least worthy of remark that no one protested against either the hardships undergone by the aged knitters of agency goods, nor against the meagerness of the pay received for the work done, and certainly no Sillertonian Thomas Hood arose to awaken the torpor of the rich by writing or singing 'The Song of the Stocking.' At all events, the amounts received, small as they were, doubtless procured a few of those creature comforts that age still permitted them to enjoy.

There were no weavers in Sillerton, but in some of the neighboring parishes, work was found for this class much in the same way as was done in the knitting department. Material was supplied by an agent, and the cloth returned to him when finished. It occasionally happened, however that, for some fault in the weaving, the web was rejected, and the value of the material supplied for its manufacture had to be refunded by the unfortunate weaver. I shall now close this chapter with an anecdote, the gist of which depends upon the custom above indicated. One day a well-known medical practitioner residing in the ancient burgh of Inverurie, while going his rounds, met an acquaintance, a weaver, who was returning from a disagreeable interview with the cloth agent, and carrying a rejected web under his arm. The doctor was not aware that Davie had made a failure, and cheerily remarked, "Weel, Davie, are ye gain' hame wi' yourwark?" Davie fancied that the question was a piece of sarcasm on the doctor's part, and owed him one for it.

An opportunity soon offered. A patient of the doctor, in spite of all that science and care had done for him, went the way of all flesh. The funeral cortege was passing along the street on the way to the churchyard, and the doctor was walking behind the hearse with the sorrowing relatives. Davie chanced to be on hand, and saw, at a glance, that his opportunity had come. Rushing forward to the astonished medical practitioner, he bawled out, loud enough to be heard on both sides of the street, "Weel, doctor, are ye gain' hame wi' your wark?" putting great emphasis upon the possessive pronoun. It was not long before the doctor took in the situation, and enjoyed it accordingly, and sitting at his hospitable table years afterwards, I had the privilege of hearing the story from his own lips.

From the doctor's unqualified merriment, I presume that he was satisfied, in his own mind, that Davie's sarcasm was, at least on this occasion, unmerited.

CHAPTER XIV

LICENSED BEGGARS THE FATUOUS AND INSANE

"Angels and ministers of grace defend us!"

Hamlet.

In the last chapter, in stating what I knew about the poor before the poor laws were enacted, there was no mention made of any aristocracy of poverty in Sillerton. We had no Edie Ochiltrees there, no King's Bedesmen, no Blue Gowns in fact no one exercising the right of asking charity within certain, or perhaps uncertain, bounds. It was the fact, however, that there were individuals who traveled as professional beggars through many of the Aberdeenshire parishes, and who, doubtless, had obtained the privilege of doing so. I recollect the occasional visits to our village of two wandering paupers. One was called Dickey Daw, a poor harmless idiot, and her companion was a middle-aged female who solicited and collected means for their mutual support. We had no analogous case in Sillerton, but such cases did exist in sonic of tho neighboring parishes, and I have in my possession a document, issued by the kirk-session of Forbes, which will clearly enough show that such were perhaps common enough. The document referred to is as follows:

"These testify that the Bearer hereof Jean Bay, Sister to Isobel Bay, Spouse to Arthur Mitchell in the Parish of Forbes carries along with her Patrick Mitchell one of their children, of about five years of age, altogether deprived of the use of his Reason and Faculties of his Body ; and his Parents being reduced to Straitning Circumstances, and having other two young children incapable thro' Nonage to do anything for themselves, are obliged to employ the said Jean Bay the Child's aunt to supplicate and beg from charitable and well-disposed Persons for the said helpless objects Sustenance and Relief. Therefore the Kirk-Session of Forbes did, and hereby do, earnestly recommend the said Jean Bay to the Charity of all within the united Parishes of Forbes and through Burgh and Land, for her own and the said great Objects Relief : which in name and by appointment of the said Kirk-Session is attested at Forbes the twenty-ninth Day of December, One thousand seven hundred and fifty-six, by, ALEXANDER OREM Moderator. Alford Feb. 24th 1757."

That the Bearer the above named Jean Bay is really an Object of Charity, as having the Burthen of the above Arthur Mitchell's Children is attested by:

ALEXANDER JOHNSTON Minister of Alford,
PATRICK THOMSON Minister at Tough,
WILLIAM MILNE Minister at Kildrummie,
FRANCIS ADAM Minister at Cushny,
THEODORE GORDON Minister at Kenethmont,
PATRICK REID Minister at Clat.

The capital letters, commas, etc., are the same as in the original. This license to beg is duly printed on a tough, dark-colored paper, and very distinctly shows tear and wear. How long it was carried about through the vale of Alford and surrounding districts to advance the claims of Patrick Mitchell and others I know not; either the imbecile boy or his devoted nurse may have died in the parish of Sillerton, and the certificate alone remained to show the miserable parochial provision existing in Scotland in the year of grace 1756 for her fatuous poor. Such documents are still issued in the province of Quebec, but lacking generally the formality of the Scotch one. May we draw the inference, that we are here, in some things at least, more than a century behind the civilization of Aberdeenshire? So much, then, for our duly accredited poor.

There were, however, two classes besides, who did not seem to dovetail into the general order of things. The fatuous, or 'feels,' as they were generally called, but not imbeciles like Patrick Mitchell, had no special place in our elemosynary system, and led a somewhat peculiar life, wandering from place to place in search of their daily bread. There was little to blame here, as generally this class was not by any means dangerous, and, in some slight respect gave, in the amusement they afforded, a species of return for what they had received, while their way of living entailed little, if indeed any, hardship whatever.

As an example of this, there was one individual of this class, one par excellence, who periodically visited Sillerton, 'feel Jamie Nuckel,' as the folks called him. I fear Jamie was more rogue than fool, and stood head and shoulders, in cunning and perhaps intellect of some kind, over his wandering confreres. Jamie had a most retentive memory, and was accustomed to repeat, almost verbatim, sermons that he had once heard. This faculty was a source of unbounded pleasure to the farm-servants on a winter evening, whenever Nuckel made his appearance, and the reward was just as much brose as Jamie could get under his belt.

On one occasion, however, his prowess in brose-consuming nearly ended in disaster. The modicum of brose provided for him was something almost incredible, and Nuckel broke the record. But he also almost broke something beside, as my father's men, who had given the dose as a test case, had to roll the glutton on the floor for a considerable time before he was considered safe from an explosion that might have proved fatal. Jamie's cry on this occasion Was very touching, "Row me or I'll rive, boys." He was rolled most effectually. That was his last sermon and feast there, for orders were given and these orders had to be obeyed that the experiment was not to be repeated, and many a time I have seen him as he passed, turning a longing look askance at the bothies of Fusselbare, where he had so often enjoyed a square meal, but his borrowed eloquence was no longer in demand in that quarter; the meal, butter, and boiling water were never again mixed for him, and Fusselbare knew Nuckel no more.

It may be well to state here that Nuckel was an exaggerated specimen of what the Poor Laws would now place under the heading of 'fatuous,' and that there were many different varieties of the same species, ranging from the unmitigated idiot, to individuals who wanted only 'tippence of the shilling.'

It is a matter of doubt if the 'crank' might not be a connecting link, and if he might not be accurately classed between the feel and the madman. It is no matter of doubt, however, that we are now getting on dangerous ground, and that a return to our mutton might be advisable. Of those who scored a few points below the ordinary standard of full reasoning powers, one, Sandy Forbes, carried a private mail-bag, to and from the post-office of Sillerton. It would be difficult to specify precisely what Sandy wanted, and I might be better understood if I said, "Just a little of everything."

Both in body and mind there was a want. One said that Sandy's fingers were 'a' thooms;' another asserted that he scuttled in his walk, 'like a fluke;' and unquestionably he had a stutter in his speech. As to his mental equipment, there was a general haziness in every department. And yet Sandy was a useful enough member of society. He was good-natured, and willing to work, so far as his capabilities went. But it was chiefly as postman that Sandy was employed. He not only carried the letters to and from the post-office, which was also the village store, but he was universally employed along the road to bring small purchases with him on his return. These small orders amounted sometimes to a very great number, but neither cash nor orders embarrassed him; he wrote nothing down, and yet goods and cash were always right, while no order was ever under any circumstances forgotten. Sometimes it happened that Sandy had been sent in another direction, and a substitute had to be sent instead, and as usual, came orders and cash from every farmer and cottar's wife along the roadside.

But what a reckoning was there on the return trip! Orders were entirely forgotten, or changed, or delivered in the wrong quarter; the guidwife of Pitfuffie found two ounces of tobacco where she expected the same quantity of tea; Johnny Wright's snuff turned out to be ground ginger that was sorely missed by a dyspeptic invalid farther on the road, who received a pound of three-inch nails instead; and in no case could the cash be brought to an exact balance. The only thing that did really seem to tally, was the universal remark made with considerable bitterness, but only when the spurious postman had got at least a good hundred yards away "I wish the peer feel, Sandy Forbes, had gane to the post instead of that gype." Here again nature seemed once more to make up in one direction what she had withheld in another, and where judgment was sadly deficient, memory was supplied with a greater liberality.

I am here reminded of an anecdote that I heard told by one who was intimately acquainted with the folk-lore of the Garioch, and who was wont to amuse many a Sillerton dinner-party therewith. The anecdote related to a family connected with the parish, and showed the difficulty that sometimes existed of determining the mental condition of an individual. A doubt had arisen whether the heir-at-law of a certain estate could be considered perfectly sane or not, and this for legal reasons. He had been guilty of no outrage against the ordinary decencies and conventionalities of society, and he was quiet and retiring in his manner, but yet legal forms required to be satisfied. A species of jury met to inquire into his mental condition, and took evidence accordingly. Several witnesses, for and against, were examined, as there were conflicting interests involved, and at length the defendant himself was brought before the Court. Several questions were put to him, all of which he answered with sufficient clearness, and the impression was growing that the verdict must be given in his favor.

Tiring of the questioning, however, to which he had been subjected, he slightly lost his temper, and asked the Court to hurry up, as the cattle would not be housed till he got home! The remark was fatal, and turned the scale that was inclining somewhat to his own side. The incongruity of the heir of an ancient house acting as cow-boy was to his judges clear enough evidence of mental weakness. The verdict was accordingly given in favor of plaintiff, and the self-appointed cow-boy lived to a good old age, but never entered upon the possession of his inheritance, and remained divested of the right and power of managing his own affairs. Of the two undesirable classes I have mentioned, the 'feel' has now been described as the representative of the one, and I shall now pass on to the 'lunatic,' as representing the other.

It is a strange thing to think of, yet not stranger than true, that lunatics, pure and simple lunatics in every sense of the word were, many of them at least, at large in 'Bonnie Scotland' about fifty years ago; not the merely fatuous, but even those who, if not admitted to be normally dangerous, might become so at any moment. Of course a wild raving maniac had to be looked to, and stone walls, and the never-failing strait-jacket, either restored the equilibrium of mind that seemed to have been disturbed, or provided another unfortunate for the funeral where there was little sorrowing, and but few tears.

The connecting link was certainly a very peculiar being, quiet generally and inoffensive, and able to speak discreetly on every subject except one; but no sooner was that one mentioned than all rationality fled, and the monomaniac came at once to the front. Examples of this class are often to be met with, but in Sillerton there was certainly a very peculiar variety of the species. James, or rather Jamie Muir, was a fine, strong, well-built chiel; able to attend to any ordinary duties, and possessed of a garden that was the admiration of the whole country-side. But Jamie was literally mad on tartans. Whether he had got the idea that he was descended from some great Highland chief, I could never learn, but on all marked occasions, when the good folks of Sillerton met for festive or other purposes, there was Muir in full Highland costume, and sporting a bonnet and feather that might have passed muster before a Field-Marshal.

One other peculiarity Jamie had; he made a practice of climbing to the top of the tallest trees in the parish, and always left a small flag of tartan fluttering from the topmost bough. On one occasion he slipped when leaving his loftiest perch, but as the tree was a larch, the branches drew out, so to speak, as Jamie's weight came upon them, and when he arrived, or nearly arrived, at terra firma, he lay upon half a cartload of branches, and the stately tree was completely stripped on one side. Jamie was considerably flurried on this occasion, but a huge pinch of sneeshin' put him all right again. Nor did the accident wean him from his dangerous proclivities. Jamie was still to be seen among the branches, like the Pygmies of Darkest Africa, and his small flags still fluttered mast-high over his favorite trees.

His brother was, however, an entirely different character. Dark in appearance solitary and unsociable in his disposition, and imbued with melancholy ideas with regard to most religious subjects, Willie Muir had more than once been placed under restraint, and had returned home, only after long intervals of absence. No one imagined that he was really dangerous, but yet there was a general desire to shun him.

On these occasions, when it was evident that the disease, if disease it was, was growing on him, Willie, or rather mad Willie Muir, as he was commonly called, was often to be seen passing through the little village, always bareheaded, and generally with a ponderous cudgel in his hand. On one of these occasions, instead of passing through the village, as was his wont, he made at once for the parish school, and opening the door suddenly, stood before the terrified youngsters, and, if possible, the more terrified schoolmaster. Looking neither to the right hand nor to the left, he made direct for the bench where sat Marshal Graham, one of the biggest boys in the school, and probably one of the most self-possessed. "Marshal Graham!" roared the madman, "take up your Bible there; turn up the fifth chapter of Mark, and read it before me, roun' the village square; and if ye miss ae word or letter, aff gaes yer head, like a carl doddie!" The carldoddie was one of those heavy-headed grasses with which we played some game of chance, by knocking off the heads against each other.

Up rose Graham, without one moment's hesitation took his Bible in his hands, duly turned up the chapter as directed, and quietly awaited further orders. With a quiet but firm grip upon the collar of the jacket, Mair speedily put Graham in marching order at the door of the school. But before the Scripture reading began, there was a preparation on the part of the madman that utterly terrorized the whole community. Muir deliberately drew from his pocket a razor, evidently prepared for the occasion, and brandishing this several times before Graham's eyes, ordered him to proceed. During all this time, which, after all did not extend beyond a very few minutes, the poor dominie seemed dumfounded and helpless, but as Muir and his Scripture reader marched away from the school door, he suddenly seemed to recover his senses, and escaping from one of the windows that opened towards the back, made for the manse as if a thousand fiends were behind him. Luckily, quiet, gentle Fordyce was in his garden, and though a peculiarly retiring and indeed timid man, lie yet at once went with the still more timid schoolmaster to the rescue of Graham.

But how progressed the reading all this time? Slowly yet firmly, Graham marched round the village square reading aloud the prescribed passage, with Muir following closely behind him, listening eagerly to the words as they fell from the boy's lips and watching if there was any divergence from the authorized text, for mad Willie Muir knew the passage most accurately, and would, no doubt, have visited an error with instant and terrible punishment. There was something supremely awful in the madman's look as he stalked behind that almost doomed boy, and brandished the weapon of punishment in his hand. Once had the square been gone over, yet the chapter was only half read, and the weird ordeal went on. At that hour there was scarcely a man in the village, and if man there was, he certainly made no sign. The terror stricken urchins did not dare to approach the scene openly, but from nooks and corners watched the progress of the reader and his judge. Ah! might not that judge at any moment have developed into the grim finisher of the law; while many a blanched face peeped out cautiously from the windows as the procession moved along, dreading at every instant lest the final tragedy might come.

On still went Graham and Muir, till the square was circled for the second time, and just at that point, as the minister and the schoolmaster reached the group, Graham's voice clearly and correctly repeated the concluding words of the chapter. There was an ominous pause, only for a second or two, and then the madman's voice uttered a responsive "Amen." The unexpected appearance on the scene of the clergyman, whom Muir had been ever taught to respect, seemed to act like a sedative upon his troubled mind, and slowly the open razor was closed and placed in his pocket. With admirable tact,

Fordyce forebore to revert to the cause that had brought him so unexpectedly to the village square, and, as he made some commonplace remarks that at once attracted Muir's attention, the sorely tried but successful scripture-reader at once took in the situation, and quietly placing a few yards between himself and the trio, suddenly put on a spurt that has probably seldom been beaten.

There was no meeting again that day in the parish school of Sillerton. The dominie was considerably demoralized, and the scholars had witnessed a scene that might have well driven Latin, and English grammar, and everything else completely out of their heads for even longer time than an afternoon. At all events, neither teacher nor taught entered again that day the school, and it was a long time before it ceased to be remembered what the occasion was that gave a half-holiday to the children of Sillerton. Mad Willie Muir had to be put once more under restraint, and never again returned to the parish. It was generally said that on his recovery he emigrated to America, while a few were wont to relate on social occasions, when talk and toddy flowed freely together about the village inn, that they had reason to believe that Muir was eventually devoured by grizzly bears among the 'Rockies' of the then 'Far West.'

Be that as it may, we believe that some social Scottish customs have been changed for the better, and that there is no great chance now of any youngster of Sillerton being paraded to read a Scripture lesson with a raving madman at his side, and with the suggestive accompaniment of an open razor blazing ominously before or behind him.

CHAPTER XV

CONVIVIALITIES OF SILLERTON

"Wi' merry sangs an' friendly cracks,
I wat they didna weary;
An' unco tales an' funnie jokes,
Their sports were cheap an' cheery."

Halloween.

It is undoubtedly a relief to pass from the company of fools, monomaniacs, and madmen to almost any other society whatever. But yet most of our pleasures are founded on contrast, or at least intensified by it.

The poet has not forgotten to remind us that 'Sweet is pleasure after pain,' and we scarcely require to go to the poet to become convinced of this truism. We seem to fall in love on some principle of contrast; the grave not infrequently affects the company of the gay; learned Lords of Session have, in more than one instance, taken to themselves wives whose chief education consisted in the ability to roast a joint or broil a beefsteak; while how often have we seen a veritable giant of six feet and a few inches over, striding along with a wife hanging on his arm who might have passed for a first cousin of one of Gulliver's Liliputiaus!

Probably it was the force of contrast that induced the comely Scotch lassie to marry, and who, when asked by a neighbor, "Fat made ye marry that ugly chiel?" very innocently replied, "Weel I wat, he's nae a beauty, but then he's sic a guid-natured breet."

Well, from the grave things discussed in last chapter we would now take a glance at those social amusements that occasionally and sometimes periodically engaged the attention of the good folks of Sillerton. No better description of the lively game of football, as practiced by the boys and hobbledehoys of the parish, could we give than that supplied by the author of 'Tullochgorum,' but alas! few Scotchmen now would get through a verse without looking into Jamieson at least a dozen of times, and I much fear, I will scarcely be held to have thrown much enlightenment upon the subject by quoting the following stanza:

"Like bumbees bizzing frae a byke,
When herds their riggins tirr,
The swankies lap thro' mire and syke,
Wow as their heads did birr!
They youff'd the ba' frae dyke to dyke
Wi unco speed and virr;
Some baith their shou'ders up did fyke,
For blythness some did flirr
Their teeth that day."

Then we had our Halloween, not perhaps with all the different ingredients that Burns with artistic hand has thrown into his wonderful poem, but yet we had many of these, as well as those grand bonfires, that in our young days lighted up every hill and brae from Aberdeen to the Moray Firth, for this much we could discern from the Mither Tap o' Bennachie; how much farther north I cannot say. Then came genial Yule with all its wealth of fun and jollity, and Auld New Year's Day, that we all sat up to greet, with its lucky or unlucky 'first foot,' its inevitable whisky bottle, its sowens, both for the comfort of the inner man and for the ruin of the door of him who had perhaps weakly allowed sleep to steal upon him, and so forgot his midnight vigil; those shooting matches that gave a deeper zest to the plowman's holiday; and last, though not least, on high occasions, the grand bull in some public hall, or perhaps barn, swept and garnished for the nonce, and where high and low met on a common platform, where all went merry as a marriage bell, and ordinary jealousies and social differences were forgotten, at least until next morning's sun threw into shade the tallow dips that still flared and spluttered on the wall. Then what of our weddings and christenings?

Were they not social events well deserving of commemoration? Who could express a doubt who mingled in our merry-makings fifty years ago, perhaps less? The christening had, of course, its higher religious associations, but it had its social side as well, and the genial parson, as a rule, when he concluded one part, was by no means averse to mingle in the other, the fact being that in Scotland, and indeed among Scotchmen wherever located or domiciled, the minister's duty was only half performed when the child was duly enrolled a Christian, and at the social board thereafter, his carving knife required as fine an edge as his tongue possessed before grace was said. I cannot deny myself the pleasure of here repeating an anecdote that I got from one of the fathers of the Church of Scotland in Canada. Would that I could reproduce the very words and gestures that give such reality to the story!

The scene was laid in Scotland, where a knowledge of the Shorter Catechism was supposed to be the property of every man, woman and child belonging to the Kirk, and where regular diets of catechising were held throughout every parish at stated times by the parish minister. A parishioner called upon his minister to request him to come and christen his first-born. The minister consented, but took the liberty, as was his duty, of asking John one or two questions in the Catechism that touched more particularly upon the question of baptism. John was found wanting, so far as knowledge on this subject was concerned, and the conscientious parson put off the christening to a more

convenient season in fact until John should call a second time at
the manse, and prove that his knowledge of things sacred was on
the increase. John duly came, but alas! no increase of knowledge
came with him, and still the minister refused to name the
baptismal day. In vain John pleaded that his brother and his
brother's wife and various relatives had been invited, and could
not decently be put off. But all in vain; the parson was obdurate.
The baptism had to be delayed; the invited guests had to wait a
little longer, and John had to compear at the manse again 'on
approbation.'

Once more John came, but frail memory refused still to
repeat the information that the Catechism gave, and on which his
wife had most perseveringly coached him, and the minister was,
if possible, more obdurate than ever. John pressed the point hard;
invited friends would be offended, and in fact insulted, and all
that sort of thing. But no; the christening must be still delayed
for reasons previously given. At last a happy thought struck the
parishioner, and he at once unburdened himself of his secret.
"Weel, minister, I may jist tell you the truth. Oor freens micht be
put aff, bit, ye see, I hae bocht the whisky, and ye ken yoursel'
that whisky winna keep."

My venerable friend did not enter into the whole scope
of the argument that John so deftly handled, nor shall I either, but
taking into account all the circumstances of the case, and after
carefully coaching his somewhat obtuse pupil in his lesson, the
worthy divine saw fit to shorten the term of purgatorial trial
through which his parishioner was passing; the christening was
duly celebrated at the time desired, and friends and whisky were
both there. As to how the good folks of Sillerton celebrated their
weddings, I presume there was little difference between them
and any other folks from 'Maidenkirk to John o' Groats.' That
little difference consisted, I believe, in a shortening- of the time,
which must have been a happy relief to the newly-married

couple, who, in those primitive days and places, did not start immediately after the 'dejeuner a la fourchette,' to spend their honeymoon among strangers, but who began to dispense the duties and graces of hospitality immediately after the nuptial knot had been tied.

There was, of course, the usual feet-washing the night before, and all the fun connected with the performance of that preliminary portion of the marriage service, and shared in chiefly by the nearer relatives and more intimate friends; there was the gathering at the bride's home of the invited guests; the bride in all the glory that such an occasion could supply; the groom scarcely knowing whether he stood on his head or heels; the bridesmaids and groomsmen wearing white gloves, and wondering what was their duty to do next; and the parson, duly robed for the occasion, and presiding not only in the more sacred part of the service, but also in the merrymaking that followed the conclusion of the ceremony.

And then what fun and frolic came! How the tables verily groaned beneath the toothsome burdens that they bore! What genial and humorous speeches were delivered as the fumes of the exhilarating toddy rose to the very ceiling of the banqueting room! What sly wit and pawky humor flowed in one continuous stream from the sharpened tongues of the merry guests; and at last, how the younger members of the community enjoyed the concluding scene of the evening's performance if indeed three or four o'clock in the morning could be so designated when the bride's stocking was thrown among the revelers, and happy was the lad or lass that had the good fortune to catch it! Their turn undoubtedly came next.

Yet, all the marriage festivities were comprised within two rounds of the clock in Sillerton, though farther north the celebration of a marriage sometimes occupied nearly a week, and came to a close, only when provisions and mountain dew were both exhausted. A near relative of mine had the privilege of witnessing a wedding a hundred miles or so north of Sillerton, where the ceremonies were all conducted in Gaelic, where the ordinary conversation was kept up in that language, except occasionally when English was employed in deference to the groom and his best man, who both spoke the Doric of the Garioch, and that only, and where my friend escaped matrimony, at least on that occasion, by what is sometimes called a 'close shave.' I shall allow him to tell his story in his own way:

"On one memorable occasion I witnessed a wedding on the banks of the Dulnan. A lad from Sillerton had found his fate beyond the Spey, and I was induced to accompany him to the home of his bride. It was a long and weary road from a few miles south of Bennachie till Craigellachie and the Hatighs of Cromdale passed, we crossed the swift-flowing Spey near Grantown, and pushed onward in the direction of the famed Aviemore. About three in the morning, in the month of May, we came in sight of our destination, but even at that uncanny hour there were no eyes closed at Carr-Bridge. One would have thought from appearances that the Prodigal Son had arrived, and that at least a dozen fatted calves had been sacrificed to welcome him. The feast had already begun, and music and dancing held high holiday.

A most cordial reception was accorded us; Oriental hospitality could scarcely have surpassed in any way the welcome that met us on the banks of the Dulnan, and though the language of Ossian was not quite so familiar to us as the Doric Scotch that we had learned not far from where 'The Gadie rins at the back o' Bennachie,' yet we felt, and had every reason to feel, that we were highly honored guests. Resisting all temptations to indulge in a Highland fling, we soon sought the seclusion of our own rooms, and had the whole and entire company of the 'Jolly Beggars' been rehearsing their celebrated cantata in the adjoining apartment, we would have remained as oblivious of their very existence as if our own mothers had rocked us to sleep. Soon too soon for us the morning dawned dawned, I mean, when the shutters were removed and the sun's rays proved that Old Sol had beaten us by at least a couple of hours.

A perfect feu de joie was being fired within an easy distance of our windows; about as many pipers as the famous Fershon paraded to conquer and ravage the Clan MacTavish seemed to be tuning their instruments in the immediate vicinity, and as your humble servant was groomsman, and deeply venerated the immortal Nelson's signal, 'England expects every man to do his duty,' we were soon ready for action. What I or anybody else did on that memorable occasion seems to have slipped almost entirely from my recollection. I know that the old Celtic parson persisted in mistaking me for the groom. I had in fact joined hands with the blushing bride, at his urgent request, thinking that this was probably the right thing for the best man to do in the land of the Grants, until a kindly hand forbade the banns, and I at once took second place, but when that marriage commenced or ended, I am not quite prepared to say.

About a week after, I had a most exciting search after my Lowland garments, having evidently donned the garb of old Gaul at a very early stage of the proceedings; and found to my surprise, by examining sundry documents that had been placed inside my sporran, that I had proposed to, and had been accepted by, over a dozen young ladies of the Strath. This, to me, was a somewhat startling revelation, and as I was not quite prepared to explain my peculiar position to all the stalwart fathers and brothers who might very soon be attempting to interview me, I beat a very precipitate retreat homewards, and as soon as possible, Craigellachie and Bennachie were by and by placed between me and the enemy. I am not quite sure why I, on this occasion, forgot so far my usual caution. It may have been the demoralizing influence of the unseemly hours we kept; perhaps it may have been produced by the extraordinary stimulating nature of the mountain air in the neighborhood of the classic Spey. At all events I never attended another wedding within a day's march of Rothiemurchus; the more staid and sober customs of a marriage in the Garioch were, like Artemus Ward's old flag, good enough for me.

I have, ever since that famous time, firmly believed in the adage, that it is unwise for the shoemaker to go beyond his last. Nay more, I had theorized upon the proverb, and began to think that it might be better for Sillerton bachelors to keep to Sillerton belles, and if I ever again consent to aid and abet a friend in entangling himself in the nuptial noose, I shall insist on a Garioch celebration, and will personally appear rather in decent Garioch continuations, than befool myself in assisting to perform the same function arrayed in the garb of old Gaul, with a Gaelic Psalm or Pibroch or Coronach, or something of that sort, ringing in my ears, and that too a hundred miles nearer the North Pole than I should be."

Such was the account that my friend gave me of his experiences at a wedding on Speyside. It will no doubt provoke a smile, his difficulty in finding a good reason for his forgetting so many circumstances connected with the celebration, as also his forgetting his Lowland caution so much as to enter into love engagements wholesale and retail. No doubt the pure air that was wafted to the Strath from the snowy heights and heath-clad sides of Cairngorm and Benmachdhui might have had an exhilarating effect upon a Garioch Scotsman, but there might have also been other causes. I once was one of twelve, who celebrated the opening of salmon-fishing on the crystal waters of the Dee by a capital dinner in one of those hotels on Deeside, that were common enough in my young days, and where nothing was wanting, in the way of either solids or liquids, to make every one as happy and contented as mortals may be. Of course, among many other luxuries, the 'Salmo Salar' played a conspicuous part.

Many good stories of the rod and reel were told ; and a few good fishing songs were sung, and could the gentle Isaac have revisited the earth, he would, I flatter myself, have felt perfectly at home among us. It is almost needless to say that at clue intervals the small thistle circled rapidly round the table, and that after the walnuts and the wine had run their course, the rest of the evening was mainly devoted to the mixing of those ingredients, that in days of old accompanied and closed every entertainment.

What we brewed or drank on that occasion I shall not specify precisely, but may simply state, that not particularly long before sunrise we all wended our way, to our respective homes. Next day we met by special appointment, and it seemed that every one had some ailment that last evening's dinner had given him not anything very serious or dangerous, but sufficient to place him 'below par.'

The salmon had disagreed with the digestive organs of several; the pudding had been disastrous to a few more, and one or two lamented that they never indulged in cheese without proving martyrs to their indiscretion the following day. One thing struck me as very peculiar, namely, that none for a moment suspected that the very liberal allowance of barley bree that they had consumed had any hand in their troubles. And yet, after all, I strongly suspect, that had a jury given a verdict upon the evidence before them, the fish, pudding, and cheese would have been declared innocent, and that a true bill would have been found against John Barleycorn. Is it possible that the peat-reek had anything to do with my friend's peculiar conduct on the banks of the Spey? I presume, after all, that the exhilaration was more due to its potency than to even the pure air of the Strath.

Times, doubtless, have changed now, but the last time I spent a few days in that quarter of the globe, a guest at the hospitable shooting quarters of a world-renowned English brewer, the first vision of the morning was the head-keeper with some genuine mountain dew to 'wash down,' as he said, 'the cobwebs that had accumulated during the night.'

When a sportsman got wearied beyond his strength, breasting the rocks and braes in pursuit of the oftentimes wild and scared red grouse, the same panacea was at hand with the remark that one spur in the head was better than two in the heel; and the last thing at night was the liquid and aromatic nightcap unfailing herald of that sweet and unbroken slumber, that in those days, or perhaps nights we should say, we never missed. Ah! well may we say with the old Roman Burns 'Tempora mutantur, et nos mutamur in illis.'

CHAPTER XVI

OTHER SILLERTON AMUSEMENTS THE SOCIETY OF GARDENERS

"I hear them still, unchanged though some from earth
Are music parted, and the tones of mirth
Wild, silvery tones, that rang through days more bright!
Have died in others, yet to me they come,
Singing of boyhood back the voices of my home!"

Hemans.

Were it for no other reason than to look up the old records of the parish, I would fain revisit Sillerton. But what records, after all, could I look into, except those of the kirk-session, and I scarcely think that I would find there anything like a paragraph headed, 'One of the amusements of Sillerton.' I might find the record, carefully and circumstantially told, of grave offenses against the laws of the kirk, and morality in general; I might learn, if I did not know before, how the kirk-session dealt with transgressors, who certainly in those days 'found their ways hard;' well and faithfully would I find it recorded that some incorrigible black sheep had to occupy the 'cutty stool,' or seat of repentance, sometimes for many consecutive Sundays, and receive the public rebuke of the stern minister, and the sour and unrelenting looks of many an old saint, who had himself, perchance, turned over a new leaf, and, clothed in his robes of self-righteousness, had forgotten the warning, 'Judge not, that ye be not judged.'

Sitting at that session table, now many years ago, not as judge or jury, but as a simple scribe wielding not the tongue but the pen; listening to sobs that came from the very depths, and seeing tears that did not merely trickle, but freely flowed over young, yet careworn cheeks, my thoughts wandered back to that grand old Temple of Jerusalem, whose greatest glory was, that it saw Him who came to carry back the wandering lambs to the sheep-fold. A woman, bowed down with grief, and perchance remorse, bends before One who traces letters on the sand, indicating probably the ease with which records of sin might or should be blotted out, and utterly disregarding the stern faces that accused their frail sister, and demanding a judgment upon her sin. At length a voice says "He that is without (this) sin, let him cast the first stone at her." The shaft has struck home, and one by one her accusers silently steal away. When the Savior looks up, none but the accused is there, and tenderly come the words from His gentle lips "Neither do I condemn thee. Go, and sin no more." Ah! how much more kindly was that erring one dealt with in the Jewish temple, than many an erring but repentant sinner in the auld kirk of Sillerton! Such scenes would, unbidden, flit before my mind, and refuse to be driven away. They relentlessly left the stamp of an iron heel upon my soul; they came to stay, and with little effort I can recall, alas! too many of them still.

Well, I might, and certainly would, find recorded, tersely and coldly, such scenes as I have hinted at, but of any mere worldly amusements, or things of that nature, no, not one line. And yet Sillerton had its gala days, when the parish put on its best looks, and work was pretty much at a standstill. There, for example, was the one great Fair that came once a year to gladden the hearts of not only the Sillertonians, but those of the neighboring parishes as well. There was, however, an object in the great annual Fair. Farmers gathered from all quarters to buy and sell; servants were engaged for the coming half-year and received the 'arles' that were as binding nearly as the Queen's shilling. Jockey was able to buy ribbons to tie up Jeannie's 'bonnie brown hair;' quarrels between rivals in the paths of love or war were either settled over a few glasses of Sillerton whisky, or decided with gloveless hands, in a fight to the finish, and according to some rules well-known to all, and which probably formed the basis of the Marquis of Queensbury's rules; and last, but not least, the annual Fair gave the boys and girls that usually Attended the parish school of Sillerton a full and genuine holiday.

We can readily see the 'why' and 'wherefore' in all this, but in the case of the great annual meeting and grand parade of the Sillerton Gardeners, I was never able to fathom the cause of their existence in any shape whatever. This society, if it might be so called, is amongst the shadows of the past, and it requires some effort to recall it very clearly. Like the shadows whose hands Aeneas attempted to grasp in Hades, and who eluded him like a flitting dream, so appear now these shadowy Gardeners to me. As Wordsworth has it in his 'Laodamia':

"Forth sprang the impassioned Queen her Lord to clasp;
Again that consummation she essay'd;
But unsubstantial form eludes her grasp
As often as that eager grasp was made."

And yet all is not mere shadow, and some figures rise above the ordinary level, like hilltops over a fog-covered landscape. The origin, however, and some other points connected with the Gardeners' Society of Sillerton, for a society it was really named, must remain, I fear, in profound obscurity. It is likely enough that when Sillerton Paradise was planned, and became an accomplished fact, with life-size figures of Adam and Eve, half-hidden among the yew-tree branches, the Gardeners may have been organized to represent some visiting committee of good or evil. This, at all events, I do know, it was at least no benefit society, but the funds and dues collected at the annual parade were simply transferred from the pockets to the stomachs of the Gardeners, the expenses of the annual dinner requiring all the funds on hand, and rendering a cash account quite unnecessary. This parade took place, I believe, about midsummer, at any rate when flowers were in their highest perfection, and in the village and neighborhood there were great preparations made for the gathering. Floral designs were then in order, and to our juvenile imaginations it seemed very wonderful, what the artistic talent of Sillerton could produce in that line. These designs were all ready the evening before, and made their appearance only when the floral warriors were ready to march.

At last the eventful day dawned. There was a distant sound of music, if not of revelry; the brass band of Oldmeldrum weavers had been engaged for the occasion, and scouts, who were out in force on such an exciting time, reported that the musicians had already crossed at Boaty's Ferry, and were now approaching the village in full blast. It would be difficult to say whether the cattle in the Druid Park or the youngsters of the village were the more impressed and delighted. I use the expression advisedly, for surely if dolphins could be charmed by the lyre of Orpheus, the bovines of Sillerton became equally susceptible of pleasing impressions at the brazen blasts of the Oldmeldrum weavers. And there in the village square stood the venerable Gardeners with flowers and banners and spears ready to receive them.

The author of the 'Siller Gun' must have had such a vision before his mind's eye when penning the lines:

> "But ne'er, for uniform or air,
> Was sic a group reviewed elsewhere!
> The short, the tall; fat folk and spare;
> Syde coats, and dockit,
> Wigs, queues, and clubs, and curly hair;

Hound hats, and cockit!
Of that the dinlin drums rebound,
Fifes, clarionets, and hautboys sound!
Through crowds on crowds, collected round,
The Corporations
Trudge off, while Echo's self is drowned
In acclamations!"

Whether there was a special costume besides the aprons that the members wore, and on which a nude Adam and Eve, the Serpent, and an apple-tree in full bearing, were all depicted in the most cunning sampler stitch that the parish maidens could supply, I know not; but there was one figure there that I remember as if I had seen him only yesterday. Sourie, as he was familiarly called from Sourfauld, the name of his little farm, seemed, for some reason or other, to have been appointed perpetual Brigadier-General. An old man then was Sourie, but still straight as a ramrod, and approaching the heroic in height. There were few opportunities for training orators in Sillerton, but had there been, Sourie would certainly have borne the bell.

I recollect some of the old man's quaint sayings, and there was a very marked difference between them and the utterances that came from his less gifted neighbors. Perhaps, were I ever to visit the churchyard of the old parish I might trace the rudely-carved lines that tell where the farmer of Sourfauld was gathered to his fathers, and not inappropriately repeat the line: "Some mute, inglorious Milton here may rest."

It is with the live Sourie, however, that I am now dealing, and as he stands there at the head of the Gardeners of Sillerton. But what a wonderful metamorphosis has taken place, and who would recognize the plainly-clad and somewhat patched tenant of Sourfauld in the towering Goliath who directs the movements of the Gardeners? The bearskin cap of a Life-

Guardsman would have hid its diminished head before the lofty headpiece that Sourie wore. Who designed it, or why it was so designed, has not been written among the chronicles of Sillerton.

The Spartan warrior who fell in battle was borne home upon his shield. Was it possible that the Sillerton designer of martial garments knew something of ancient history, and moved by the careful thrift of his own countrymen, and profiting by the recollection of Spartan adaptation, so constructed the helmets of our local warriors that, should the wearer fall in battle, he might be easily and economically buried in his capacious headgear? A bright scarlet coat, somewhat resembling what our fighting forefathers wore about a half-century before, covered the greater part of the elongated form of the commander-in-chief, and partly concealed a pair of gigantic boots that resembled very much those worn by swashbucklers in the time of Cromwell, while a remarkably long sword completed the outfit, so far at least as my memory warrants a description. Whence that sword came has often been a source of wonder to my boyhood days. Could it have been found near Wallace Neuk in the brave toon o' Bon-Accord?

Might some local antiquary have lent it for the occasion, or did the village blacksmith, in a moment of high warlike spirit, design and fashion the terrible weapon that, like the helmet of Navarre, blazed as a guiding star in front of the Gardeners, who now, to the clang of martial music, tramped around the village square, and four deep, marched straight through the shady walks of the home park to the House of Sillerton, the residence of the Honorary Chief of the Gardeners, and where the commander-in-chief and his men went through a species of royal salute? Poor Sourie! when I recall the old man to my memory, I think of him as Oliver Wendell Holmes thought of his so-called 'Last Leaf ':

"I know it is a sin
For me to sit and grin
At him here;
But the old three-cornered hat,
And the breeches, and all that,
Are so queer!"

On the conclusion of these preliminary exercises, prizes were given for the best floral designs, slight refreshments were handed round, the patron's health was drunk in a bumper of good Scotch, three ringing cheers were given, and to the inspiring music of the brass band, whose whistles had now been duly moistened, the Ancient Gardeners wended their way back to the village. Probably the gentle reader may here be ready to say, "We are done with the Gardeners now." Not by any means. The parade is over, flags and spears, and aprons, drums, fifes, and swords are laid aside, but the real business of the Gardeners of Sillerton is now only beginning.

I have heard it said, that after all, the Gardeners of Sillerton were incorporated simply to enjoy a dinner once a year in the roomy dining-room of the Gamut Arms. This may or may not be the case, but I certainly knew one individual who joined the society for this special object, and for no other. 'Protty,' as he was nicknamed, was one of the characters of the locality, and while usually leading a sober and industrious life, yet, on high occasions, got somewhat befuddled, and on the occasion of the Gardeners' dinner got gloriously fou. Protty, like Lazarus of old, got few of the good things of this life, but he determined that at least once a year there should be an exception to the rule, and cheerfully paid his annual subscription to enjoy the coveted luxuries of the annual dinner.

And what a dinner was there! The season for haggis had not yet come, but haggis was quite a common dish in the locality, and did not exercise that influence upon the salivary glands that it does upon Scotchmen in foreign lands, who meet to en joy that great national dish once a year, namely, on the natal day of Scotland's patron saint. But beef and greens were there; mighty rounds fit to set before a Queen; fish, fowl, and all the et-ceteras that in those days went to constitute a feast that was required by, and demanded too, a vigorous appetite, It was verily 'strong meat for strong men.' But how much of these luxuries fell to the lot of poor Protty? The fact was that the wags of Sillerton and their name was 'Legion' knowing Protty's relish for good things, had so ordered it that not one of the luxuries should reach, in Protty's case, their legitimate destination. Protty was able, during the progress of the dinner, to enjoy the nips of whisky that followed, or perhaps accompanied, certain courses, but a dish of mashed turnips, heavily sweetened with sugar, and replenished again and again, was all that Protty was permitted to enjoy, Protty being too obfuscated by repeated libations to see the trick that was being played upon him.

Such was one of the standing, practical, and perennial jokes that were relished in those days, and doubtless very heartily laughed at by those who cheated the Ancient Gardener of his due. That all this was very reprehensible who will deny, yet, personally, I feel no responsibility. I promised to paint Sillerton, not as it should have been, but simply as it was, and I doubt not there are some yet among the denizens of the parish,who, if they ever cast their eyes upon this page will remember well the stalwart frame and honest, homely speech of the leader of the Ancient Gardeners Sourie of Sourfauld; and as they revive the story of the mashed turnips the only dish partaken of by the fuddled Gardener will not the phrase the well-known, the oft-repeated phrase be repeated again Protty! Protty! Sandy Mackie?"

CHAPTER XVII

THE WARS OF THE ROSES

"'Spare our comparisons,' replied
An angry Rose, who grew beside;
'Of all mankind you should not flout us;
What can a poet do without us?
In every love-song roses bloom;
We lend you color and perfume.'"

John Gay.

Fear not, gentle reader ; the humble historian of
Sillerton's quiet ways has no intention of appropriating the pen of
a Macaulay or a Napier, and whisking you off to the great
battlefields of Ilindostan or of Merrie England. A theme more
becoming an Abercleensliire chronicler, were he martially
inclined, might be found nearer home, and doubtless he would
find a suitable subject for his talent in the "sair field o' liarlaw'
When Donald came branking down the brae Wi' twenty thousand
men."

Our 'Wars of the Roses' were simply the friendly
competitions that took place at the annual meeting of the
Gardeners of Sillerton, between our rival horticulturists, and
where the rose, par excellence, played a very prominent part.
Indeed, before dismissing the parade of the said Gardeners, if I
have not already done so, I have one incident more to relate,
without which my narrative, to me, at least, would seem
incomplete. I have already remarked the extraordinary interest
that the Gardeners' Day excited both in village and district. The
local amateur horticulturists and there were several such in the
neighborhood, who, in addition to success in growing their

favorites, possessed the art as well of arranging them in beautiful forms and combinations had a peculiarly deep interest in the day.

Apart from the pleasure that success would bring, there was, in addition, the satisfaction that the money value of the prizes won would also afford. And thus there was a double stimulant supplied. Secretly each competitor formed his plans and carried them out. No State secret was more jealously guarded than his, and no rival, or indeed anybody else, would be allowed to obtain the faintest glimpse of the mere skeleton that now, bare and uninteresting, would, on the great marshalling day of the Gardeners, stand in the Sillerton Square arrayed in all the beauty that a rainbow robe of exquisite flowers would lend.

Truly Solomon in all his glory was not arrayed like one of these. The interest also was of a double character, and that of the competitor was shared by all the boys of Sillerton. We had each of us our favorite, and him we were pledged to aid and abet to the best of our ability. I fancy I hear one saying "But in what way could aid be given?" Well, that is an easy matter to explain.

While the embryo floral crown, or whatever device it might be, was complete in every part complete in so far as the mere skeleton or framework could be called complete yet its flowery robes and adornments must needs be all added on the morning of the parade. And thus we became jackals to the lion. We arranged beforehand with non-competitors, who would, early on the morning of the eventful day, give us the gleanings, nay, the whole yield, of their gardens. The friend who provided me with my floral tribute was known in the parish by the name of General Hay. Let me now introduce the old man. Upwards of six feet in height, at least fourscore years of age, yet unbent by time or infirmity, the General has anticipated our errand, and is already in his garden awaiting our arrival. He greets us kindly, and smiles as he marks the number of baskets we carry, for I had secured a partner in the carrying business, and the said baskets conveyed the gentlest of hints that our demands upon his flower-garden would not by any means be of a modest nature. I believe, however, he took this as a compliment, and had he been possessed of the Oriental 'Gardens of Gul,' or been entitled to glean Mount Hybla's roses, he would have culled every flower, rather than send us away unsatisfied. As to the old gentleman's habiliments, a pair of knee-breeches, with long tight stockings, and buckled shoes, as a continuation, finished his outfit as to the lower extremities, and showed a pair of long, thin legs that harmonized admirably with his 'tout ensemble.'

The coat had a half military look, showing a very capacious and high collar, and extending nearly to his knees. The well-buttoned vest did not allow much of his breast linen to be seen, but this was more than equalized by a remarkably high shirt collar that rose above the ears. I never saw such another but once, when I made one of my first visits to Aberdeen. The amount of cloth around the individual's neck induced me to ask his name, and my companion informed me that the wags had named him the 'British Linen Company.' But I seem to have forgotten the head-piece, and left that to be last described which generally should claim first notice. 'Cap-a-pied' with me seems to have been reversed, but I shall take the reader into my confidence and tell why I adopted that course. It may be possible that I was thinking of Robert Browning's Christmas Eve, and that personally I might be a twin brother, at least in spirit, of that...

> "Artist of another ambition,
> Who, having a block to carve, no bigger,
> Has spent his power on the opposite quest,
> And believed to begin at the feet was best,
> For so may I see, ere I die, the whole figure!"

The fact was, however, that, like the small boy, I kept the

sweetest morsel on the side of my plate for the last mouthful. The bon bouche was an excellent close to the feast. It was not exactly the Glengarry cap that attracted my attention, for the General in this respect resembled Rob Rorison:

"It wasna the bonnet, but the head that was in it,
Made every one speak o' Rob Rorison's bonnet."

And so with General Hay not the bonnet, but the head itself, attracted the attention. The last 'queue' that was worn in Sillerton hung from that head. I had often seen the 'queue' in pictures that represented a generation that had almost passed away, but on the living subject, with this one exception, never.

Why General Hay clung to this relic of a past age when all his contemporaries went 'shaven and shorn,' it were hard to say, and supplied a problem to the young antiquaries of the village that was never solved. But there it was, and in the church on Sunday, where its owner was always in his place, it attracted more attention, I fear, from the younger members of the congregation than the somewhat dry yet classic utterances of the staid and stately Robert Fordyce. It was as well a matter of no small curiosity to me to know how Hay had received his 'soubriquet' of General, and it at least proves the prevalence of that vein of fun and humor that existed in Sillerton, and which, so often, as we have seen, came to the surface. All the small boys associated old Hay with scenes of carnage and blood, and no doubt believed that he had played no unimportant part in the military history of the country. Personally, I was reluctantly undeceived, and learned from an old sergeant of artillery, whom I often visited to hear his account of battles in the Peninsula, in which he had taken a part, that the old man had never seen nor heard a shot fired in anger. When the Scottish youth enrolled themselves members of the Militia that prepared to meet any threatened invasion, Hay found himself a full private in a

114

company of which the junior lieutenant owned the same name as himself. To what particular branch of the family Lieutenant Hay belonged it would be difficult now to say, as the Hays were decidedly a fighting family; many of them rose to distinction in the army, and if Generals there were among them and undoubtedly there were will not their names and deeds be all duly recorded in the military annals of Aberdeenshire?

When the rumors of war and the smoke of battle cleared away, Private Hay converted his spear into a pruning-hook, and condescended to cultivate cabbages and roses in a quiet and cozy nook not far from the gate of Paradise. The warlike Lieutenant decided otherwise; buckled on his sword the more tightly, and went to fight his country's battles wherever and whenever fighting was required. Step by step Hay rose in rank in his profession of arms, until one day the news reached Sillerton that the whilom Lieutenant was now General Hay. For some reason or other, now unknown, and queer though the idea may seem, yet the good folks of Sillerton insisted, in an overflowing fit of fun and frolic, on raising their own peaceful Hay to the same rank with his more warlike namesake. In fact he became, in one sense, the military hero's 'Double-ganger.' The *soi-disant* Lieutenant Hay of Sillerton became eventually, after passing through all the intermediate gradations of rank, General Hay, and General Hay he remained to the end.

He never resented the courtesy that gave him rank, and responded to his title as naturally as if he had won it on the field of battle. He was a kindly old man, and ever sent us small boys away infinitely pleased with our reception, and loaded with the beautiful treasures of his garden. May his ashes rest in peace! His memory to me is still as fragrant and fresh as the sweet-scented roses that he once grew. The Sillertonians, though brimful of fun, yet invariably left it behind them when they visited the resting-places of the dead, and yet, incongruous as it may seem, I often wonder if they carved the name 'General' on his tombstone in the churchyard of Sillerton. Having begun this chapter with unmeasured eulogies of the rose, I fear that the unwarlike General Hay led me away from my first love, and that the peculiar circumstances that gave him his tinsel rank, and the charms of a peaceful life, that made him supremely happy among his flowers, made me almost forget the prominent part that the rose, whether or white, or damask, played in the Gardeners' competition in Sillerton.

I shall at once acknowledge the guilt, and make the only reparation in my power, by closing this portion of my reminiscences in the following, though very slightly altered, lines of the immortal Keats:

> "I saw the sweetest flower wild nature yields
> A fresh-blown musk rose; 'twas the first that threw
> Its sweets upon the summer; graceful it grew
> As is the wand that Queen Titania wields.
> And as I feasted on its fragrancy
> I thought the garden-rose it far excell'd;
> But when, oh, Hay ! thy roses came to me,
> My sense with their deliciousness was spell'd;
> Soft voices had they, that with tender plea,
> Whisper'd of peace, and truth, and friendliness
> unquell'd."

CHAPTER XVIII

PRACTICAL JOKERS AT WORK

"Take thy beak from out my heart, and take thy form
from off my door.
Quoth the raven, Nevermore."

Poe.

While not going quite so far as the Aberdoniau who is reported by Max O'Rell as saying, "Tak awa Aberdeen and a few miles roan' aboot it, and whar are ye?" I yet cannot forget that in the shire, at least, of Aberdeen there was a vast amount of that species of wit in my boyhood days that found a ready outlet in practical jokes, as I have had occasion frequently to note in this picture of Sillerton life that I have been attempting not to paint but to reproduce. Protty Sandy Mackie was not the only victim that was bagged by the Sillerton jokers, but I shall contrive to give one or two instances that came under my personal observation, and which I shall attempt as well to narrate within reasonable limits. That the village store, or shop as it was then called, should be a common rendezvous on a Saturday evening goes without saying, and there, accordingly, both buyers and sellers convened ; stories were there told, and there practical jokes were sometimes perpetrated that, as we shall see, occasionally left indelible marks behind them. The shopkeeper, or merchant, as he was designated in those days, was a man of considerable energy in his calling, and did not confine his attention altogether to the ordinary style of doing business.

In fact, the merchant came of an enterprising family, and showed it in more than one way, as his transactions proved. One Saturday evening, when the store was pretty full of customers served and to be served Mr. Baggs informed them that he had made a fortunate venture in the way of foot-gear, and in consequence was prepared to sell boots at a price that would strike dumb the souters of Sillerton. The goods were there and then produced, and so well did they look, that sales to a considerable extent were at once effected. A near relative of mine was there, but he had made no purchases. Being asked if he would not invest in a pair of boots, he stated that he would rather deal in a different way. He said in fact, that he would much prefer to take his boots by the year, or, in other words, that Mr. Baggs should take a twelve months' contract, and keep him in foot-gear during that time for a certain amount, the said amount to be then and there agreed on between them.

This proposition being somewhat novel, was received with great applause by the crowd generally, and was at once favorably entertained by the merchant, whose heart was considerably opened by the number of sales he had effected that evening and the profits realized. The sum was, after a little haggling, settled ; the terms were agreed to, and a note was at once drawn up defining the terms of the agreement, signed and duly witnessed. I remember quite well one or two of the conditions. One was that a boot might, if it required such repairs, be only twice soled and; after the second soling to become the property of the wearer. Another was that no patch whatever was to be placed on the uppers, but that, when such an operation became necessary, the dilapidated boots were to be returned to the merchant and replaced by a new pair. There was much merriment over the novel contract, but as the price to be paid seemed large for a twelvemonths' wear of boots, the laugh was clearly on the merchant's side. How the laugh turned to another quarter we shall presently see.

My friend was employed in the Garioch district at a considerable distance from Sillerton; he returned home every

Saturday evening, and I usually went with my pony to meet him the greater part of the way, when we contrived to get home by the well known process of 'Ride and Tie.' I now, however, got instructions to no longer make my usual Saturday trip, as my friend intended walking until his boot contract was finished.

The first Saturday night came, and with it came Dick, as I may call my relative, who, after supper, speedily found his way to the village store to have his boots examined. They were pronounced seaworthy by the referee, but there were deep traces of tear and wear that went to Mr. Baggs' heart. It was evident that another trip beyond Bennachie and back, with nearly a week's work thrown in, would change considerably the rating of Dick's boots. The 'A 1.' would certainly go down the scale. Another Saturday night came, and Dick and his boots came also. The weather had been bad; the distance to be traversed was long; the roads were execrable, and the fears of the shopkeeper were fully realized, for two new soles had to be ordered from the village cobbler, while Dick marched off in triumph with his feet snugly encased in another pair of Mr. Baggs' boots.

It is needless to say that this process went on much in the same way till the end of the twelve months. The story meantime had got wind, and every youngster who could find an excuse for purchasing the smallest article contrived to be in the village store just about the hour when Dick generally put in an appearance, and almost invariably with a pair of dilapidated boots.

Everybody enjoyed the chagrin of poor Baggs, who was the butt of the parish for a twelvemonth and more, and no happier man was there in Sillerton than he when the boot contract was eventually and finally closed. Curiosity tried hard to worm out of Baggs the exact state of his account in this boot transaction, but the village shopkeeper declined to respond; silent was Baggs as a very oyster; he preferred to keep his own secret, and the village bookkeepers succeeded in arriving only at an approximation. It was well known, however, that the balance was on the wrong side of 'Profit and Loss,' at least so far as Baggs was concerned. Probably a Yankee might have guessed that the boot was on the wrong leg. The only one that had reason to regret the closing of the boot-contract was my pony Donald. When Baggs' boots ceased to be worn on contract, Donald's services were on demand once more, and Saturday afternoons now found him no longer enjoying his ease in his cozy stall, but on a return trip from the back of Bennachie, and alternately carrying on his back his light-weight master, and a somewhat sturdier rider, who no longer wore boot s supplied by contract, and who now enjoyed a 'lift' on his Saturday trip homeward. After all Baggs was only a little in advance of his age, and was a true type of those who sell everything, from a 'needle to an anchor,' and who would feel ashamed were they unable to supply on demand an umbrella or a sentry box.

> "He had a fouth o' auld nick-nackets,
> Rusty aim caps and jinglin' jackets,
> Wad haud the Lothians three in tackets,
> A towmont guid,
> And parritch-pats and auld saut-backets:
> Before the Flood."

CHAPTER XIX

THE WINNING LEG

"Ae market night
Tarn had got planted unco right;
Fast by an ingle bleezin' finely,
Wi' reaming swats that drank divinely."

Tarn o' Shanter.

Had I the intention of being mysterious, I could scarcely have adopted a better heading to this chapter than I have done. The winning card might be easily understood, even in the quiet village of Sillerton, where a friendly rubber was played by the upper ten in the manse parlor or in the gentlemanfarmer's drawing-room, and where 'catch-the-ten' was the favorite game among the lads and lasses of the parish, with a touch 'of old maid' now and then indulged in, just to vary the entertainment. The winning horse might also be understood, when farmer bodies, with sharper spurs in their heads than on their heels, occasionally tried the mettle of their nags.

But the winning leg was out of the ordinary run of the village vocabulary, and would have puzzled a Sillertonian as much as a quadratic equation would have done a celebrated Aberdeen professor, who never got past the golden rule of three, but whose fervid eloquence has roused Scotchmen to enthusiasm from John O'Groats to wherever Scotchmen are known, and that means the 'warl' ower.' Well, it will be in order now to explain, but I claim the privilege of telling my story in my own way. As was said in a previous chapter, the Inverurie markets, which I think were of monthly occurrence, were a source of pleasure and profit to the business folks of Sillerton, and groups of these, mounted on their bob-tailed nags (for the blood horse had scarcely yet become a favorite among our rugged hill roads, and the gig or phaeton was put into requisition only when ladies were in the case), were to be seen trotting along quietly and doucely towards the ancient burgh.

I would not say that the pace homeward in the evening was quite so quiet and formal, but this might be easily accounted for by the fact known to every naturalist, that the horse on the home-stretch is a much fleeter animal than when his head is turned away from his own oat-bin. The Rev. Sydney Smith, of happy memory, who lived for years in Edinburgh, where there were literary giants in those days, and who yet gravely asserted that it would require a surgical operation to get a joke into a Scotchman's head, was a close observer of human nature, as we may judge by the above assertion, and carried his observations also into that of the equine family.

Sydney was well aware of this propensity of the horse to hasten towards his own oat bin, and so ordered it that, in the case of a horse he possessed, the oat bin should be ever before him, 'Calamity' had defied all efforts or whip or spur to accelerate his movements, and Smith at last hit upon the happy expedient of fastening a small vessel containing a feed of oats upon the end of an elongated shaft. This worked as a veritable charm, and the witty parson was borne along at a rattling speed, while the very sight of the golden grain before the eyes stimulated the craving steed to redouble his efforts to overtake every moment what he eventually reached only when he got home. It may be at the same time quite possible that what added to Tam o' Shanter's courage, may have helped the Sillerton farmers to shorten, at least by time, the trip homewards from the Inverurie monthly market. In fact it was pretty widely known that farmers generally returned home from these markets pretty well corned, as the saying was. Nor was it looked upon as in any way strange that such should be. Opinion, indeed, leaned exactly in the other way. I once heard a very peculiar exemplification of this. A well-to-do farmer was boasting that he at least had never come home from market in that happy and exhilarated state. His wife, a lady of the highest culture, and certainly one of the leaders of fashion in the parish, but withal possessed of a considerable amount of homely Scotch humor, very naively replied to her husband's boast, "Well, George, and if you did sometimes, I would not think a bit the less of you." Did it follow that she would have thought the more?

I often joined the cavalcade as a matter, not of business, but of pleasure, and if I did not learn much about the price and quality of different sorts of grain, nor of those agricultural questions that were often keenly discussed, even in the saddle, I yet gleaned some knowledge of human nature, that may have sometimes helped me in after-life. On our arrival the horses were usually stabled at a well-known hostelry within the burgh, and there, towards evening, when all market business was at an end, the riders met to enjoy the stirrup-cup before mounting their nags for the homeward ride. Maybe strict veracity might suggest that cup should be used in the plural number, as there were occasions when Tom Ledingham's blend rendered it somewhat difficult to leave the table just at the end of the first tumbler. Stories, too, did not always quite fit the emptying of the glasses, and the equalizing of the two things often cost time and money both, when an 'eke' had to be taken to get ends to meet. One evening matters were precisely in this stale, and a Sillerton farmer, to twit mine host of the Elphinstone Arms, would persist in telling funny things about Inverurie, and, among others, a story of one of the local clergy who had preached lately in the neighboring church, very soon after the close of a keenly-contested election of bailies and other officials for the burgh.

Things had not gone precisely in accordance with the minister's political views, and probably he would have preferred to take no notice whatever of the magistracy that now sat very conspicuously before him. The custom, however, was, in the closing prayer, to pray for those in authority over us, and custom in the Auld Kirk was like a law of the Medes and Persians, 'it altered not.' The minister duly conformed to the custom, and pray he did, but in a way that doubtless failed to excite the admiration of the subjects of his supplications, "God bless the Magistrates o' this ancient burgh, sic as they are."

One roar of laughter from the Sillertonians greeted this anecdote, and mine host had to own that the tale had been truthfully told. One story led to another, one of which referred to feats of strength that the narrator had witnessed, and this probably tempted the landlord, who was a man of ponderous dimensions, to wager a bottle of hot Scotch, that his leg would measure, round the calf, more than that of any man in the company. At first no one seemed inclined to take up the challenge, but at length a farmer who lived near us, and who was certainly the smallest man in the room, called out, "Tarn, I'll tak' your bet, man." Sim Eddie was our neighbor, and I quietly attempted to dissuade him from his rash offer, but to no purpose. He was resolute, and I was appointed judge or umpire. The landlord's leg was produced mid duly taped, and from appearances no one doubted but that little Sim would have to foot the bill, for no one thought that he could possibly leg it. Nothing daunted, Sim in turn presented his leg for measurement, but, ye gods ! what a leg was there! We were all amazed, and any measurement seemed unnecessary, but yet the tape had to do its duty, and Eddie's leg took two inches of the line more than Tom's. This settled the matter, and the bottle of hot Scotch was a free stirrup-cup to the fanners of Sillerton.

As we rode homeward I could not help wondering how it was possible that so small a man should have so large a leg, and, sidling up to the winner of the bet, I plumped the question, "How does it happen, Sim, that you have so big a leg?" The honest farmer answered me at once:

"Weel, laddie, I'll jist tell you. Ye'll recollect I had ance the scarlet fivver, an' got a1 richt again; bit the dregs o't settled in that leg. That's jist it; bit eh, man, wasna I frichtened that I wad hae to exhibit the ither ane, for as sure's death it's a perfect spindleshank!"

The reader may readily conceive the merriment that rose at the explanation. But the joke did not end here exactly. It oozed out over the whole countryside, for Ledingham was well known throughout the bounds of the Garioch, and the badgering he got over that leg-wager was enough to kill any ordinary man.

It worked, however, in a different way with the host of the Elphinstone Arms. In fact, Ledingham nearly killed two commercial travelers who had carried their quizzing rather far, and after some time it came to be understood generally, and particularly among the farmers of Sillerton, that, in the matter of the 'Winning Leg,' silence was golden, and would undoubtedly prove a winning card, at least in one of the hotels in the neighborhood of Inverurie.

CHAPTER XX

THE MINISTERS CHRISTMAS DINNER

"And now farewell each dainty dish,
With sundry sorts of sugared wine!
Farewell, I say, fine flesh and fish,
To please this dainty mouth of mine!
I now, alas, must leave all these,
And make good cheer with bread and cheese!"

Breton.

The Rev. Robert Fordyce, minister of Sillerton, was a douce, sober man in every way the last man in the world to poke fun at anybody, and the very last, certainly, who should have been the victim of a practical joke. The festive season was now approaching, and his reverence had been duly invited to eat his sixtieth Christmas dinner at the hospitable table of a parishioner, the tenant of Milton. Invitations in those days did not contain the cabalistic letters, 'R.S.V.P.,' but yet the Reverend Robert had forwarded his acceptance, and had every intention of honoring the entertainment with his presence.

The guidwife of Milton soared somewhat above the ordinary run of farmers' wives. She had seen a little of the world beyond the boundary line of Sillerton, and she dearly loved, on occasion, to see a choice company enjoying themselves round her groaning mahogany. And so the minister and a few other favored ones were invited to eat their Christmas dinner at Milton. But here it behooves us to introduce another character upon the scene. No minister was ever complete without his man, and even the Scriptural fox-tail story could scarcely have been told, without a minister to preach, and a minister's man to whistle. Gentle reader, allow me to introduce to you John Sprot, the minister's man. John, indeed, was no ordinary man.

From boyhood he had served the clergy, and if not yet arrived at the years of discretion, certainly from the influence of precept and example he should have reached that goal long ago. John had, in fact, become manse and glebe property, and in that capacity had described a circle, a sort of ecclesiastical circle, throughout the bounds of the Presbytery, until he now found himself general manager for Mr. Fordyce of Sillerton, delving in the manse garden, cultivating the glebe generally, and when his master, who was no Jehu, held his annual 'catechizing' throughout the parish, or once on a while accepted an invitation to dinner, driving him in the old gig that had now for more than a quarter of a century been the admiration of the little boys of Sillerton. But just here the question naturally arises Why had not Sprot settled down in one favored spot?

Why was John still a rolling stone that gathers no moss? Well, there is a delicacy in the answer that the writer of this humble narrative feels keenly, but yet the truth, the sober truth, must be told. John Sprot was, in fact, a ___, no, I don't exactly mean that, but while John was a strong advocate of temperance, yet the flesh was sometimes weak, and so it happened that, on a few occasions, John had been what Scotch folks kindly call 'overtaken.' The consequence of this was that when his reverence then weighed his man in the scales of sobriety, and found him wanting, pastures new had to be looked for, and another manse door closed behind him forever. During, however, one of John's escapades, an accident had converted one of his seemly legs into something resembling an arc of a circle, and while this gave him a most peculiar style of perambulation, even in his soberest seasons, yet it was generally believed that good would come of it, and that his conduct in the future would be as straight as his lower member was crooked.

127

A whole year, last Martinmas, had come and gone, and John Sprot was still the minister's man of Sillerton. If temptation had come, it had evidently also been successfully resisted, and the more observant of the villagers had begun to express an opinion, that John might close his earthly career in the cozy manse of Sillerton. Alas! how weak is human nature at best but no, we must not anticipate. The day of Milton's dinner-party came, and, if great preparations were made by the guidwife of Milton, the minister's man was far from idle. Under the genial influence of soap-suds and an abundant supply of elbow-grease, the ancient gig had actually renewed its age, and the old gray, through the persuasive action of a new curry-comb, had parted with a few pounds of that fur which, if it increased warmth, at the same time very materially diminished speed. John felt somewhat exhausted with his unwonted exertions, but experienced a keen satisfaction in the reflection that man, horse, and gig were ready for action. Seating himself upon an old wheelbarrow that stood invitingly near, he contemplated with considerable satisfaction his work, and, as he lighted his pipe, and began to feel the influence of the subtle narcotic, he felt supremely happy, and it is at least doubtful, had the change been possible, if at that moment he would have exchanged places with the Reverend Robert Fordyce of Sillerton.

Just then a small callant that ran messages about the village appeared on the scene, and intimated to John, that Marshal Graham, now manager of the Sillerton distillery, requested to see him with the least possible delay. Graham was a confirmed practical joker, and seldom did a week pass without some new cantrip on his part that set the whole country side roaring with laughter. Sprot, impressed with the seeming importance of the message, hesitated not for a moment, but at once proceeded to the office, where he was received with marked courtesy. Graham informed him with the utmost gravity that last night he had been grossly insulted by the land steward, James

Power, and, knowing John's character for probity and caution, he requested him to carry to Power a note demanding an immediate apology, failing which he said he believed the matter would end in bloodshed. John was considerably dumbfounded by this startling intelligence, but a sense of the confidence placed in him, along with a horn of Sillerton's best dew, nerved him for his delicate mission, and away he went to deliver the somewhat hostile note. Having read the threatening message, Power pretended to get into a terrible passion, tearing the letter in pieces and swearing that blood alone could settle the dispute between them. A reply was instantly penned, and, charged with another horn of the same generous sedative that he had swallowed only a few minutes before, John soon placed Power's note in Graham's hands.

The fact was, that the two worthies, knowing that the minister was due that evening at Milton, conceived the brilliant idea of putting John Sprot hors de combat, and so spoil the parson's dinner, seeing that it was an established fact that the old gentleman could no more drive a horse and buggy, than he could have directed the mano3uvres of an ironclad. Back and forth went Sprot; letter after letter wits written by the two belligerents, horn followed horn with the now decidedly obfuscated minister's man, until Milton's Christmas dinner had passed from his memory like a flitting dream. The barley bree that makes some men pugnacious, only softened the teuderest sensibilities of John's heart.

He fancied that he was engaged in the noble work of pouring oil on troubled waters; without his individual efforts, human blood might have been shed, and, feeling thus, we fear the malt got aboon the meal; the heartless jokers were only too successful, and the apostle of peace fell before the syren blandishments of Sillerton's ripest mellowest purest mountain dew. But where was the Reverend Robert Fordyce all this time?

he had seen the earlier exertions of his faithful servant; he had watched from the manse Windows the marked progress of John's work; the old gray looked as if the vagaries of colthood might be again assumed; the antiquated gig reminded the douce parson that correct truly was Keats when he penned the line :

"A thing of beauty is a joy for ever,"

And dreaming of no malign influence to cross his path, he resigns himself to pleasing waking dreams of many a merry Christmas that he had seen and kept, before the manse was still and lonely as now; when childish voices and pattering feet were wont to reach unchallenged his own quiet snuggery, and before he had known what it was to read a portion of one's own history on the mossgrown stone that he could even now see from the study window. But dreaming will scarcely clothe the minister of Sillerton for his Christmas dinner. And so he bestirs himself anew. The decent broadcloth becomes his rounded figure well; the shirt front, heavily ruled, looks like the driven snow; a chain, resplendent with keys and seals, passes to and forth across his breast, and with feet encased in warm overshoes, and closely buttoned in a ponderous overcoat that two maiden daughters arrange lovingly around him, the Reverend Mr. Fordyce smiles kindly upon his surroundings, and, passing through his hall to the graveled walk in front, takes his first step in the direction of his Christmas dinner.

But where was John Sprot now? Where the renovated gig? Where the rejuvenated gray? The minister peers curiously towards the manse stables. He sees something approaching, but not precisely what he expected. The horse and gig were just as they should be, but, alas! John Sprot, the minister's man, was where no minister's man should be, at least when under orders to drive his master to a Christmas dinner. John had been placed, by officious hands doubtless, upon the back of the gallant gray, but there was assuredly a bar-sinister in his surroundings his face was towards the tail, and two callants, who had evidently been engaged for the occasion, were trying as best they could, to enable the driver to preserve his equilibrium, and to direct at the same time the movements of the astonished gray towards the manse door.

One glance at the strange procession was enough for the minister, who quickly sought and found again the privacy of his own chamber; the now irate maidens divested him of his more outside coverings; the immaculate black was speedily exchanged for less pretentious garments; and instead of the savory turkey and ham, with all the et-ceteras that filled and adorned, that evening, the groaning table of the tenant of Milton, our douce minister was perforce content to dine on a cold joint that had done duty on the manse table the day before. How the gig, the gray, and John Sprot (we here, for conscientious reasons, reverse the order of precedence) found their due and allotted places I know not. I do know that John awoke the day after Christmas 'a sadder but a wiser man.' This, however, was a season of mutual forbearance; forgiveness was asked and found, the merry wags were inclined to own that they had carried the joke a little too far, and in after-years, when the Reverend Robert Fordyce dispensed, on special and favored occasions, the blessings that covered his own table, he sometimes condescended to tell the story, with a slightly sad and pensive smile, how it happened that he missed his Milton dinner, on that now long-past Christmas day.

I need hardly say that Sprot's escapade was not so quickly forgotten by the jovial Sillertonians, as it was forgiven by the kindly minister, and the jokes that were cracked on the occasion, and the excruciating quizzing to which John was subjected, could scarcely be borne by the victim with genuine equanimity. The fact also that it occurred at a time when conviviality was in order, drew more attention to it than had it happened at a busier season, and often at bachelor dinners, long after, have I heard a song sung, recounting John's Yuletime adventure, that local talent had both composed and set to music. There were three stanzas of this song, two of which my memory had faithfully retained; one had irrevocably, at least so far as I was concerned, passed away. An esteemed correspondent, however, living near the locality, arid who, when very slightly prompted, recollected all the circumstances of the case, sent me the missing verse strange to say, the only one he could call to mind. I am thus able to supply the three verses, which, perhaps, are curious enough to prove of interest to individuals fond of 'folk-lore.'

The music I am unable to give; I believe it was as original as the song. The loss of this, at the same time, is less to be regretted as the poetic effusion is not likely to occupy a place on the programs of many 'musical entertainments.'

I give the song, chorus, etc., as I heard them of old, only eliminating a few words that were slightly harsher than modern taste is now inclined to employ:

JOHN SPROT:

"Great Johnny Sprot, the parson's man's
A man o' muckle pith,
Wi' his fall, lall, derattle, tall,
Fall, lall, deday!
Gin ye except the crookit leg,
He's soun' in limb air lith,
Wi'his fall, lall. derattle, tall,
Fall, lall, deday!

As Johnny Sprot gaed o'er the burn,
He tram pit on a snail,

Wi' his fall, lall, derattle, tall,
Fall, lall, deday!
Then up got Johnny's crookit leg,
An' in the burn he fell,
Wi' his fall, lall, derattle tall,
Fall, lall, deday!

The minister cam' stappin, oot,
Says, "John, far are ye, man?
Wi' yer fall, lall, derattle, tall,
Fall, lall, deday!"
Says John, "I've trampit on a snail,
An' d ine bit I've faan,
Wi' my fall, lall, derattle, tall,
Fall, lall, deday!"

CHAPTER XXI

SILLERTON'S BURDENS

"Go, therefore, now, and work; for there shall no straw be given you, yet shall ye deliver the tale of bricks."

The Israelites in Egypt.

I recollect distinctly an old friend of mine illustrating well the remark that we have all, in some respect or other, something to trouble us. Two elders of the kirk were engaged in a friendly controversy, one urging that we all have some trouble, the other as stoutly insisting that some seemed to have no care whatever. During the discussion of the knotty question, which occurred as they walked along the road, a well-known 'feel' Jamie hove in sight. "Now," said the one elder, "I am ready to wager that Jamie has no trouble in this world whatever."

The other as doggedly disbelieved this, and meanwhile the 'feel' drew near. "No." says he who believed in Jamie's perfect happiness, "hae ye onything to trouble ye, Jamie?", "Fint a thing," quoth Jamie, and was passing on. "Bide a wee," says the other; "is there naething ava, Jamie, that bothers ye?", "Weel," replies the 'feel,', "John Tamson's bubbly jock leads me sometimes a sair time o't fin I'm gaen up the road.", "Ah!" said the believer in universal sorrow, "ye see everybody has his ' bubblyjock.'"

Gentle reader, this axiom or postulate was true also of Sillerton, for Sillerton undoubtedly had its 'bubbly jock.' I do not here refer so much to the village, in this case, but rather to the farmers of the parish. It was true that the villagers had found no royal road to affluence, nor did they expect to find it. They earned little, but their wants were in proportion to their means, and many of them, no doubt, felt like a celebrated New York divine, who, Socrates-like, was accustomed to stand periodically before one of the magnificently-filled windows of Broadway, and fervently thank the Lord that there were so many things in that window that he could do without. Now the plain folks of Sillerton felt like the parson, without requiring to see the window. Certainly, in their case, where ignorance was bliss 'twere folly to be wise, and they were ignorant at least of greater wants, and hence were contented.

But among the farming community there was a slightly altered state of things. The common laborer scarcely hoped to lay past more than the merest trifle for a rainy day. The farmer aspired to something higher. He employed capital in his efforts to live, and he expected, not only to be able to pay his half-yearly rent, but also to have something besides on the right side of the 'profit and loss' account. Nor was the farmer, on many of the larger estates, disappointed in his expectations. It is related that Lord Aberdeen (the Premier Earl, I mean), when he met Her Majesty on her way to visit him at Haddo House, was accompanied by about four hundred horsemen. The Queen inquired who they were, and was informed that they were a portion of his tenantry. Expressing surprise that farmers could be so well mounted, his lordship explained that he would be ashamed to have a tenant on his estate who could not afford to keep as good a horse as he owned himself.

On the Richmond and Gordon property also a like liberal policy prevailed, and indeed on many or most of the large estates; but on smaller properties things were managed in a different way, and if there were wanting the Irish 'middleman,' yet the small Scotch laird extracted from his almost helpless tenant a considerably larger 'tale of bricks' than that to which he was, in right and justice, entitled; and hence the anxiety and care and actual suffering that were so often the farmer's lot, and which were the natural consequences of that iniquitous system of 'rack-rent' that, alas! was so prevalent.

In Sillerton, successful farming was difficult of realization. Rents were confessedly high perhaps a little too high but the so-called Game Laws were the veritable 'bubbly-jock' of the parish. No farmer on the estate, or in the parish, which in this case were synonymous terms, had the right to keep even a collie dog; no farmer was allowed to use a gun over his farm; and no farmer might trap or kill a hare or even rabbit, under any circumstances whatever no, not in his own kail-yard.

Nor was this merely a negative condition, for by the terms and conditions of his lease, he was bound to protect these, and woe to him who failed to fulfill his duty in this respect. Were I imbued with the genius of a Mark Twain or an Artemus Ward I might pause here simply to moralize, and prove that the good Laird of Sillerton was acting only in a true Christian spirit, and that his leases, small codicils to the Gospels, made his tenants better Christians, in that they were not only admonished, but even compelled, to love their enemies the rabbits, and to do good to even the lower animals that never ceased, night or day, to eat them out, root, stock, and branch. Personal tastes also may have influenced the leases, for the Laird was an ardent lover of game; he did not enjoy wandering for hours over his preserves without firing a shot, and he had as little wish to see his invited guests subjected to a like trying experience.

The expression 'invited guests' leads me to note the fact, that, so far as parishioners were concerned, no one, no matter his education or social status, was ever invited to cast a fly upon the rippling waters of the 'Bonnie Don,' to try his luck with a freshrun salmo salar, nor had he ever the chance to bag a snipe or moorfowl in the company of the Laird and his guests, the latter of whom came generally from England to spend a short holiday among the heather, or who belonged to the more aristocratic families of the district.

A few boys about the village plied their trouting rods over one or two mill-dams in the neighborhood, and were never challenged for doing so, but had we ventured a cast on the Don, we should have soon come to grief at the hands of the game-keepers. We also contrived to make respectable baskets occasionally by a process we called 'knittlin' probably the boys call it 'tickling' now. We lay down on our faces close to a narrow stream, spreading out our arms to their utmost stretch, and while drawing them together, below the bank, we felt gently for trout, until our fingers creeping headwards, reached the gills. This point reached, they closed like a vice upon the victim, and the finny beauty was transferred to the creel. This was a small privilege that the Laird allowed us, and yet it was of considerable value afterwards to the boys who enjoyed it. We manufactured our own rods; we constructed our own reels 'pirns' we called them then; we wove our own hair lines, and with a peculiar knot, deftly tied, we made our own casting lines. Kay, more, we prepared our own flies.

To the skill we acquired in doing these things I have often been indebted when some dire mishap broke in pieces our 'tackle' on some lone Canadian lake, where many miles of weary portage-road separated us from skilled labor, or when the coquettish trout refused to be lured by a fly that had changed from bright scarlet to deep blue, until the exasperated angler began to assume the color of his own spurious fly. On such occasions an hour of work handicraft, I should say learned on the banks of the Clyon-dam, made rods, reels, or lines as good as new, while a few tufts of the feathers of the scarlet Ibis, replacing the dismal blues, soon changed the aspect of affairs; the fisher's sun of Austerlitz shone out once more, the sweet music of the reels began to ring again in our ears, and the speckled beauties of lake or stream quickly exchanged their native element for the shady corner that had been prepared for them in our birch bark canoes.

It may not be out of place also to own, that while neither the village nor the parish sportsmen were invited to join the battue which, at the proper season, was held on our hills, and among our tree covered and bushy 'heughs and hows,' yet the youths of the village had a way of obtaining sport, without any invitation whatever. When we wanted a white or black rabbit and such were occasionally seen in the warrens we seldom failed to find what we wanted; and with a couple of boys on each side of a 'dry-stane dyke,' with eyes as keen as a pointer's nose, we generally succeeded in carrying home a few trophies of the chase. We conducted our operations in rabbit hunting, however, on the still principle; we cooperated together, not by words, but by signs, and we never reached our homes until our distended jackets would no longer, in the growing darkness, be likely to attract attention, while the few stones that we had displaced in securing our game were more likely to be charged to the ruthless hand of time, than to any action that might be deemed an infraction of the Game Laws. Some owners of game lands were not so conservative as he of Sillerton, and occasionally gave their tenantry, or at least a number of them, an opportunity of trying their skill with the hares, rabbits, and moor-fowl. This was considered a great compliment, and was heartily enjoyed by the participants in the sport.

I am compelled to own, also, that I have known invitations issued, I do not mean in Sillerton, not exactly to afford the tenantry a day's pleasant outing, but to give the gamekeepers an opportunity of marking individuals who, through skill in using the gun, and other 'wrinkles' that indicate the sportsman, might be considered dangerous to game preserves, and who, in consequence, might be judiciously shadowed. For the correctness of this statement, I shall relate a short anecdote in illustration.

One autumn I was spending a few holidays with a well-to-do farmer, not far from the Vale of Alford. There was a prearranged meeting of the Chess Club of the district on hand, and we played chess for about three days; I might be nearer the truth by saying three days and nights. At last I struck work at the chess board, and told my host that there was no more chess for me for the next week. I said this, I believe, as if I meant it. "Weel," said my accommodating friend, "try the gun instead. I hae the richt frae the laird to sheet ower the haill fairm."

I looked surprised that he should have the privilege of shooting over his farm, which, along with a hundred acres or so of good arable land, included within its boundary-line a very large expanse of hill land, where he fed a few hundred sheep. My expressed surprise was satisfied with the following explanation, which I shall repeat in his own words, if possible:

"Ye see, oor laird disna aften tribble his estates wi' his presence, bit, aboot twa years sinsyne, he cam' doon frae Luiinun, an' efter an ook's leesure, he sen's oot invitashuns to ilk ane o' his tenants for a day's sheetin'. My neebor Whitie an' mysell gat invitashuns like the Live, bit we jaloosed that there wis something in the thing that we didna jist clearly unerstan', and sae we keepit at hame. Weel, the upshot wis that the keepers, cannie chiels, pat their keel on a' the loons that were gey skeelie wi' the gun, while Whitie an' I gat permits to sheet whenever we liked."

I need scarcely say that I gladly availed myself of Newkeig's 'permit,' and, in consequence, made a few good bags along the heathery sides of the great Grampian range.

The jealous care exercised by the Laird of Sillerton over the preservation of his game, and the unlimited means at his disposal of increasing their numbers indefinitely, could end only in one result. That which happened in Australia in later years with imported rabbits, which multiplied to such an extent as to jeopardize the crops of those portions of the Colony where they had been placed, happened long before in Sillerton. The red deer could occasionally be seen browsing among the grain and turnips; the beautiful and fleet roe might, every hour of the day, gladden the heart of a Landseer had he decided to extend his professional rambles to the parish of Sillerton, and hares and rabbits, moor-fowl and black-cock fed, and sported, and crowed as if the better part of the parish were their own. And so it was.

Forty or fifty hares were often to be seen at one time, and on one turnip-field; the grouse came in clouds to claim their share of the harvest; the deer were almost as tame as sheep, as they browsed on the richest pastures of the farm, and, to crown all, flocks of pheasants, housed, tended, and fed and pampered with assiduous care, often left a field of grain almost as worthless as if a hurricane had swept over it. And he who, by every right under heaven, owned those pastures, who sowed them, and who should have reaped those fields, would have us soon thought of joining a Guy Fawkes in a new Gunpowder Plot, as of firing off a blunderbuss, or even a pengun, to drive the voracious harpies away.

It is true that the Laird and his friends made, at the proper season of the year, heavy bags on the fields and moors; it is true that a few bucks occasionally bit the dust before the unerring tube, it is true that as many as thirty thousand rabbits had been trapped or shot in the parish during one year, and yet there was no appreciable relief to the poor game-eaten farmer. One tenant alone, a gentleman born and bred, resisted the good Laird, and attempted to protect his crops from the ravages of the rabbits. Alas! In vain. His farm was intersected by belts of woodland, among which to enter, to follow up his destroyers, would be counted a trespass and punishable by a fine; detectives were placed to mark if the obnoxious tenant overstepped the limits of his own farm, and, after a time, a conviction of hopelessness came over him, and his futile attempts at self-preservation ceased.

His lease came, a year or two after, to a close, and the farm was no longer for him; the gentleman farmer did not thrive under the Upas shadow of the Laird of Sillerton; a fitter and more plastic tenant was found in a mannie that wore a Kilmarnock bonnet on Sunday, and who, it was understood, had made affidavit that he had never fired a gun in his life. In consequence of damage received, and for which no compensation could be recovered, leases were often abandoned, but then only after the wolf was at the door, and few left Sillerton of their own accord, without having met with losses through the abuse of the Game Laws losses that had crippled their finances for years, aye, sometimes for life. Things, I believe, have changed, even in Sillerton. The gentlest creature that God has created, when driven to bay, will at least put forth an effort in self-defence, and downtrodden, long-suffering Sillerton awoke at length from slumbers that had continued too long.

Men were at last found willing to 'bell the cat,' the bundle of sticks was repeated, joint action did much to ameliorate the condition of the game-eaten farmer; competition for farm leases lessened as the channels of emigration widened, and the Juggernaut of 'Game Protection' that once rolled over a thousand Sillertons throughout Scotland, crushing, maiming, grinding beneath its mighty wheels many a noble and manly heart, many a sorrowing, despairing woman, many a suffering child, lies low as that Dagon that once fell crushed and broken before the Ark of God.

Well might our children ask us if such things could have been; and well might strangers wonder whether or not the narrator of Sillerton's 'burdens' was indulging in dismal romances, instead of delineating a truthful tale.

Simple truth was promised in my preface, and simple truth alone fills every chapter, and fills this chapter as well.

On facts too well known I take my stand, and defy contradiction of any kind, and from any quarter. There are hundreds of witnesses, still in the prime of life, who could corroborate every syllable I have written here, and were I standing now in that 'Auld Kirkyard,' I might point to more than one grave and say Had the whole truth been carved on these humble stones, their story might have read thus"

"DONE TO DEATH
BY
THE LAIRD OF SILLERTON
AND
HIS GAME!"

CHAPTER XXII

NON-INTRUSION THE NIGHT BEFORE THE BATTLE

"Oh! what a parish, a parish, a parish!
Oh! what a parish was drucken Dunkeld!
They hang'd the minister, droon'd the precentor,
Pull'd doon the steeple, and fuddl'd the bell."

Old Song.

I have no intention whatever of entering into the arena of Church politics that agitated Scotland for many years prior to the 'forties,' and which in 1843 culminated in what has been called the Disruption. It was certainly a hardship that any patron exercising the right of patronage over a church or churches possessed the power of giving the cure of souls in the Church, where he exercised this right, to any probationer to whom the Presbytery had given a license to preach the Gospel, and whose life had been unpointed at by the finger of scandal. It might have indeed been urged that it was almost impossible for any one to enter the inner courts of the Church of Scotland, who was unacquainted with those marks of erudition that had been considered indispensable in completing the education of the scholar and the gentleman.

It might fairly enough have been held, that no one of immoral character could continue to inscribe himself a probationer of the Kirk ; and it was specially provided that the ministers of the Church of Scotland had to be, like the Paschal lamb, without blemish. And yet, notwithstanding such safeguards, it was quite possible that one might be forced upon a congregation who was obnoxious to the great majority of those who, in the event of his settlement over them, must of necessity

143

listen to his teachings, and pay due respect to him as their spiritual adviser. This undoubtedly was a state of things most devoutly to be avoided, but for all that, it may have occasionally happened.

It was, however, as unquestionably true that sometimes, and more particularly near the period of the Disruption, extraordinary external influences were often brought to bear to induce Church members to ostracize a presentee, who, had no such influence been employed, would have quietly entered into possession of the duties and emoluments of his office without any hitch whatever. Sillerton had changed somewhat ecclesiastically since the days when Louis Alexander Daff failed to put in an appearance in his father's pulpit. Both sire and son had ceased from their labors, and church and school were occupied by strangers. The Reverend Robert Fordyce whom we have occasionally met before this in this narrative, was a quiet, unassuming man, quite satisfied with things as they were, and by no means of that volatile nature that the smallest spark of excitement might fan into flame.

Non-intrusion, therefore, did not make much progress in the parish, and, with the exception of a friendly discussion of the question in the shoemaker's workshop or the more commodious smithy? We knew remarkably little about events that were bringing some sections of the religious world to an incandescent heat. That Mr. Fordyce would stick to the Establishment went without saying, and as the Laird would not allow a tenant to harbor even a collie dog for fear of disturbing the game, it was not at all likely that he would give much countenance to men who were wielding every influence in their power to upset the present state of things. One or two 'Weeklies' came to the parish, but few conned their pages, and these few were not very favorable to the advocates of change. A considerable revolution had, however, taken place in our educational department. The old type of dominie had passed away, and a new one had come in, lacking many of the peculiar characteristics of the old masters, but yet full of admiration for a system that had educated men who, in popular opinion, could walk from Aberdeen to the Wall of China without meeting with any difficulties in the way of unknown tongues.

These new pedagogues loved learning on its own account, and soon began to awaken an interest in the youth of the parish, who looked forward to the probabilities of a college course, and perhaps a professional career beyond. Among half a dozen youths then, scanning their Horace, advancing cautiously through Greek sentences, and beginning to master the difficulties of Euclid and algebra, the burning Church question was at all times welcome, and the arguments that were wielded on one side or the other were all duly weighed and gravely considered nay, ofttimes argued as well. Without, however, entering into polemics; without discussing the 'Veto Act' or marking out the beauties or defects of methods that had been recommended to pour oil upon those troubled waters that thereafter obtained the designation of the 'Ten Years Conflict,' I shall at once come to what may be termed the crowning point of our ecclesiastical troubles the 'Culsalmond Riot.'

There were doubtless grievances connected with the law of patronage, and there were rights belonging to Church membership that were utterly ignored, and, to remove the one class and secure the other, a torrent of burning zeal had rolled over the land like a mighty stream, that half measures were as powerless to stem as was Mrs. Partington's broom to sweep back the waves of the Atlantic. In Sillerton we knew that trouble was to be expected. It was not certainly known that there was on the program a 'Riot at Culsalmond,' but it as certainly was anticipated that the settlement there would be anything but peaceful, while it was also pretty generally believed that the parishioners would, on the day of settlement, be reinforced by sympathizers who would leave no means untried to prevent the settlement from taking place. We shall here epitomize the circumstances of the case. There was a vacancy in Culsalmond a sad one certainly and the Presbytery of Garioch had decided to induct the Rev. Mr. Middleton, assistant to the late incumbent, and the patron's presentee, on the eleventh day of November, to the church and parish of Culsalmond. Now, seeing that the late incumbent had been deposed for drunkenness, it might have been a wise thing to have settled there some man of more than ordinary ability and parts, who might have gradually undone the evil that his erring brother had contrived to do. But this, of course, was not usually a matter of interest to the patron, who, if lie presented the son of an aspiring tenant to the living, conferred a lasting favor, and occasionally replenished his own depleted pocket-book. Whatever was the cause, it was well known that the Reverend Mr. Middleton was not by any means the choice of the people. At the same time, the Presbytery were precisely in the position of a judge who had to pass sentence in accordance with existing laws. The judge had no jurisdiction over the framing of laws, but had simply to act in accordance with such as had been placed upon the Statute Book.

And so with the Presbytery of Garioch; they were not the framers of laws, but simply the executive. The presentee of Culsahnond came before them armed with the legal documents that proved his position, and as soon as the Presbytery were satisfied as to his learning, character, and divinity, and no relevant objections were offered and sustained, there was but one course open to them. The Presbytery of Garioch therefore decided to induct Mr. Middleton on the eleventh day of November, and appointed the Reverend George Peter, of Kemnay, to preside on the occasion. From rumors that had reached Sillerton that the parishioners would, by fair or foul means, resist the settlement, a fellow-student and I thereupon resolved to put in an appearance at Culsalmond on that eventful November day. Only fourteen miles or so separated us from the field of expected battle, and the day before found us, about its close, in the village of Old Rayne, where we arranged to pass the night.

Brussels, the night before Waterloo, was not more moved than that quiet village the night before the Culsalmond settlement. Alas! no Uryside Byron has arisen to perpetuate in song what then transpired. Speedily it seemed to ooze out that two Moderates, youths certainly, had come so far to see the conflict that was likely to take place the following day. Old Rayne, unlike Sillerton, was strong in Non-intrusion sentiment, and soon its champions appeared, prepared to do battle for the great cause. I have now but a dim, a very dim recollection of the debate that followed. We two stood alone against the Rayne warriors, and did battle for the Auld Kirk as best we could. It was, however, a hard fight, and when I think of it now, after these long years, I feel considerably surprised to think that two mere schoolboys could have held their own against the sturdy common sense and genuine wit and rustic irony that were employed against them. Truly the race is not ever to the swift, nor the battle to the strong.

Notwithstanding, however, the points we made, and the foes we routed, we began to weary of the apparently interminable nature of the contest. Just then a happy thought seemed to strike my comrade, who was at least four or five years my senior, that it was full time that the discussion should come to a close, and that ordinary reasoning was evidently not the weapon best suited to foil our opponents. Suiting himself, therefore, to the exigencies of the case, and the course of action lie had resolved to take, he quoted from Acts that never existed, and from speeches that had never been made, to prove the stand we had taken, and the result was startling. Day, date, and the ipsiss-ima verba, were quoted, and as there were no documents on the spot available to rebut the statements advanced, the result was very gratifying to us, and the enemies of the Kirk were smitten, 'hip and thigh,' like the Philistines of old before the irresistible prowess of Samson.

Someone might naively hint here, 'And by the selfsame weapon.' Nay, gentle reader, not so; that debater made his mark where Dugald Dalgetty got his learning in Marischal College, Aberdeen and if any one who reads this page feels in any way anxious to know who routed the Non-intrusionists of Rayne, let him look into the chronicles of that famous seat of learning, and among the first bursars between 1840 and ten years thereafter he will find the name of my comrade.

Verily, had he been so inclined, he might have become Senior Wrangler of some celebrated English University, as he was undoubtedly first wrangler in the quiet village of Old Rayne on that eventful evening in November; but his lines fell to him in other places.

We were eventually left in possession of the field; the baffled disputants one by one disappeared, and we were anything but sorry that it was so. Ten miles over country roads had made a few hours of rest peculiarly desirable, and the tension, of the tongue-and-mental struggle with the champions of Non-intrusion, had been like the last grain of sand that broke the camel's back. Supremely happy were we when we found ourselves alone; few preparations were needed to compose our weary limbs for the couch of rest; and the ringing sound of the last hobnailed boot had scarcely died away on the cobble-paved street of Old Rayne ere our heads rested on our pillows, and we were folded in the soporific arms of Morpheus.

CHAPTER XXIII

THE CULSALMOND RIOT

"Whyles on the strong-wing'd tempest flyin,'
Tirlin' the kirks."

Address to the Deiil.

Next morning found us ready for the road. It was a cold
November morning. Bennachie had donned his white mantle,
and snow-flurries, with occasional showers of hard, biting hail,
greeted us as we wended our way towards the Church of
Culsahnond, which stood on an eminence that tested well our
staying powers, ere we conquered the 'stey brae' that lay
between.

If company could help our cold tramp that morning or
forenoon, we should rather say, as we intended to reach the
church some time between 11 A.M. And noon we certainly had it
to our hearts' content. From the farthest corners of the Garioch,
men and youths, moved by patriotic fires, or simple curiosity,
advanced in the direction of Culsalmond. The whole district
from Kintore in the southeast to parishes far beyond the Glens of
Foudland was deeply moved, the elements of combustion were
already kindled, and the volcano was ready to burst forth on the
heights of Culsalmond.

The day was too cold for continuous disputation;
generally we trudged on in dogged silence, and in duo course we
reached our destination and seated ourselves on an old
tombstone near the church. So far as I can recollect, there was no
house of entertainment near, but it seemed as if Scotch caution
had provided against all contingencies, and that not a few were

149

enabled, by the help of a little mountain dew, to refresh the inner man after their long and arduous walk, and to kindly temper to the shorn lambs (God save the mark!) the biting showers that still swept over hill and dale. Deep speculation was at work as to what the Presbytery would do. But, judging from the show of legal assistance that was exhibited around the church and manse, there was no doubt but that Mr. Middleton's settlement was to be proceeded with. One thing to me seemed remarkable. The more prominent firebrands, as we learned from a parishioner, were almost all strangers. Perhaps Culsalmond was not a forcing-house for orators. Be that as it may, the parishioners, I observed, said very little.

They were pretty generally opposed to the system that placed a clergyman over them, no matter what their feelings were; but against the presentee personally I heard not an evil word spoken, and the future abundantly proved that their action that day proceeded more from a conviction of principle than from a point of feeling.

I have said 'their action,' but there was little, if any action on their part that day, and what was done then to entitle the guardians of the peace to afterwards call the circumstances connected with the settlement 'The Culsalmond Riot' was done principally perhaps entirely by outsiders. One epithet of contempt I heard frequently applied to Mr. Middleton 'Teetaboutie.' The expression awakened roars of laughter and shouts of merriment. Yet, strange to say, the expression was utterly meaningless in itself, and was simply the name of a place where the presentee once lived. I have frequently observed that in Scottish song, sometimes the pathos depends, not so much on the sentiment expressed, as on the voice lingering sympathetically on perhaps a single word. What, after all, is in our well-known and really charming song 'Robin Adair' to melt us to deepest sympathy or even tears? And yet, when the simple refrain lovingly wails forth from the very depths of the heart, few songs can be more touching.

Now, it was just so with Teetaboutie. In the word itself there was nothing. If meaning there once was, that meaning had probably died out, even before the last Druid performed his rites in the shadow of the 'Maiden Stone.' And yet, after hearing Teetaboutie uttered by the human voice that day in all its possible inflections whispered by the young, rising like a slogan-yell from the capacious throats and lungs of the sturdy plowman, and again quavering from the thin and pinched lips of men bowed down with years and hoary with age uttered through almost a round of the clock uttered in all the notes of the gamut, from low 'G' to almost any conceivable height above, and in all its multifarious tones, expressing only deep contempt and irony, one may easily enough imagine what the effect might be.

Had the tenant of that famous place offered the writer of this the usufruct of that farm, free of rental, and insisting only that the recipient should bear the name, as all Scottish farmers do of their farms, the only reply would have been an unmitigated "No!" Having now discussed Teetaboutie in all its bearings, I shall again take up the narrative.

It is now past eleven, and at noon precisely the members of the Garioch Presbytery intend to enter the church. The crowd, however, had no idea that such an entrance should be effected, and to carry out their purpose they closed around the church doors. No Roman soldier linked his shield more closely with that of his comrade, when assaulting some ancient wall, than 'shoulder to shoulder' stood those sturdy Presbyterians who that day blockaded the church doors of Culsalmond. At last, after some legal or ecclesiastical formalities had been attended to, the word passed along the line, if it may be so called, that the Presbytery were moving towards the church. The answer was a shout of defiance and an additional squeeze, as if some gigantic python had got another coil of his tail around you, until you began to be in doubt as to how much more pressure you could endure.

The Presbytery of Garioch now approached very close to the condensed crowd, but in this case 'Tommy didn't make room for his uncle,' and it looked at one time as if the blockade was not to be broken. One, however, of the County Constabulary had taken in the situation, and succeeded in carrying his point. He was a small man physically, and divesting himself of his uniform, which might have opposed his progress doorward, he somehow contrived to worm his way, without creating suspicion, to the desired spot. A quiet and unnoticed turn of the key and the blockade was broken. The first motion of the human mass cost that constable a fractured rib, but beyond a sharp cry of pain we knew nothing. We were sensible of a slow grinding motion that was in unceasing progress; we faced sometimes the gable of the church and sometimes the everlasting hills; we were conscious of a compressive force that was almost unbearable; we had no power whatever to alter, in the very slightest degree, the course we were involuntarily taking, but we saw and felt that we were approaching slowly, but surely, the open door. With hands high overhead, and with feet innocent of contact with the gravel or grass that lay beneath them, that door was reached. That particular moment, amid all my subsequent experiences and wanderings, has never been forgotten. If two hundred pounds upon the square inch was what I endured before, there were at least a thousand as I slowly rolled past one of the doorposts.

Not more swiftly does the tensioned string regain its normal condition when the tension ceases, than my corporation came back to its original form. I seemed to shoot forward as if an old resuscitated catapult had propelled me. But, in fact, there was a double propulsion. The one was produced by a species of vacuum in front, and the propelling power behind; the other sprang from that principle of love of life that stimulates many of the forces of the human mind. But, to explain- no sooner was I within the door than a sound struck on my ear that precluded all other sounds whatever. That there was a perfect pandemonium there, may go without saying. The roar of a flooded cataract was nothing in comparison to the mingled sounds that were heard within that building. And yet the distinct crack of a beam overhead was louder still.

With the agility of youth, stimulated by the spur of fear, the top of a pew was reached, a few bounds left the cracked and still cracking gallery behind, and with a careful eye to the possibilities of falling stars and things of that sort, I speedily found myself in a window, and considered that I was as secure from the evil chances of war, as any one might well be while he remained under that roof. From my perch I could now look with some equanimity upon things transpiring about me. I am not aware whether or not the Moderator ever ascended the pulpit steps. It would have been an act of supreme folly to have even attempted such a thing, as both stair and pulpit were already occupied to repletion, and as the uproar that raged on every side would have precluded the possibility of any human voice being heard, were it loud as that of an African lion.

Patiently, very patiently, the members of Presbytery kept their usual places beside the pulpit foot. Nor was this an easy or desirable task. The ceaseless roar of angry and determined men, irritated the more by their failure to debar the clergy from the church, was not the only disturbing element there, but pieces of wood, of stone, and of lime were being thrown in every direction throughout the building. And well did the Presbytery of Garioch stand the test. There might have been differences of opinion as to the goodness of their cause; there was but one with respect to their bearing1 under such peculiarly trying circumstances, and that was one of general admiration. Personally, I was prejudiced in favor of our clergy, but I could not look that day upon their calm, determined bearing without thinking of their Covenanting forefathers preaching to their scattered followers amid the mosses and moors of troubled Scotland, where the sabers of Claverhouse's dragoons might at any moment have ended both preaching and life together. Such, thought I, were our fathers once, and such are their sons now. After waiting for a considerable time for a patient hearing, the members of Presbytery withdrew in a body from the building, and sought the quieter rooms of the neighboring manse, where the settlement of the presentee was legally and ecclesiastically consummated.

The storm that raged, however, within the walls of the church was not hushed to rest when the clergy left it. 'Holy Willie's Prayer' was given from the pulpit by special request; ribald songs were sung by the excited and sometimes inebriated plowmen; the bell never ceased its jowl until the shades of evening were coming down upon the church and churchyard, and not until almost all the chief actors had left the manse for their comparatively distant homes, did the revelers pause in their weird-like work, did the smoke of hundreds of pipes cease to roll forth from the shattered and glassless windows of the now dilapidated building, and did that old bell abandon a lugubrious refrain that has never been rung again, and we sincerely hope may never again,on the world-renowned heights of Culsalmond.

A few days afterwards I attended a wedding in the neighborhood of Sillerton, where the Reverend Robert Fordyce officiated. It was, of course, well known that he had been at Culsalmond as a member of the Presbytery, and that while on his way home the day following, and not very far from the village, some slight accident happened to the horse, and, in consequence, minister, man, and vehicle got landed in the ditch. A friendly parishioner and his plowman who witnessed the accident kindly came to the rescue, and, with some little difficulty, all were, like John Gilpin's hat and wig, soon again on the road. The father of the bride was somewhat dull of hearing, but on this occasion he seemed duller than usual. The fact was that the old farmer meant to quiz the minister and succeeded. Three times I heard the question put, "Far war ye comin' frae, minister, the ither day fin yer beastie fell i' the ditch?" As often the answer came, but in rather subdued tones. The fourth 'speerin' brought a reply that was heard all over the room, "From Culsalmond, sir! from Culsalmond."

The smothered titter that rippled through the well-filled apartment showed that the shot had told, and the good-natured host, showing only a merry twinkle in his eye, did not pursue the conversation. Another clerical friend of mine in after years was not so reticent as to things that transpired at the riot, and more than once induced me to tell the story. I had seen him leave the manse of Culsalmond on that eventful evening, and, as a number of rustics attempted to bar his way along Her Majesty's highway, he leaped his horse into a turnip field. Here he was rather closely followed for some distance by the rabble, but, being well mounted, he got a slight distance ahead, and at last saw his way clear to the highway again. Wheeling his panting nag towards his pursuers, he lifted his hat, made a profound salaam, and rode away. This was too much for his tormentors. One cheer was raised, and the chase ended. This story he delighted to repeat long years afterwards, and that exciting ride through that stiff turnip-field gave him, in its remembrance, more delight than the recollections of the best sermon he had ever preached. Such are we all; such is human nature everywhere.

I saw the carriage of an aristocratic member of Presbytery also leave the manse under difficulties. A shower of something harder and larger than hailstones damaged considerably the 'Dalrymple Arms' on the well varnished panels, but the equanimity of the occupant was in no way disturbed. In conversation afterwards the gallant baronet explained that an ordinary shower of stones was not likely to intimidate a man who had lived for years with only a sheet of gray paper between him and the infernal region.

In the witness-box some short time afterwards, the undaunted elder further explained, that he had spent several years of his life in latitudes where volcanic eruptions were almost of daily occurrence. Before closing this chapter I cannot fail to remark the peculiar tendency of the Scottish mind to express its feelings in verse under circumstances of an exciting nature. The several ecclesiastical movements that preceded the Disruption of 1843 seemed to arouse this tendency to action.

I have in my possession several specimens of what were once called 'Culsalmond Psalms,' and they exhibit no small amount of fire and sarcastic humor. I presume, however, that, as in the case of the letters of Junius, the same remark as to the authorship may be repeated *Stat nominis umbra.*

In my own case, while still in my teens, I was once guilty of a slight act of indiscretion in turning into rude verse the ludicrous adventure of a love-sick well-known breeder of Aberdeenshire cattle. It was never intended that the little 'jeu de esprit' should go further than the dining-room table, but the retentive memory of a listener immortalized what should have been committed to oblivion. Next market day, the song was said and sung through the ancient burgh of Inverurie.

Nor was it cast as a waif upon the world, for the paternity was willingly owned by one who that day reaped a golden harvest from its sale. I can recall still the sturdy upper-country poet, opening his musical campaign on the forenoon of a market day. Clad in home-spun, the stalwart Glenlivat man tossed the loose end of his plaid over his shoulder, and, stepping forward, half sung, half recited rhymes such as the following;

> "I'm John Milne frae Livat's glen;
> I wrat it doon wi' my ain pen.
> Over the mountains, over the main,
> Ridin' thro' France, and gallopin' thro' Spain;
> Skippin' the mountains like a craw,
> And o'er the hills to America!"

Such was the poet who claimed my verses, and sold them, too. Unlike the great Roman Virgil, I left the perpetrator of 'petty larceny' to enjoy his gold and his laurels in peace, but sometimes in after years, when I have heard a verse or two of my effusion quoted, doubtless a very sinister smile may have played around my lips.

It is possible that even, now after so many years have come and gone, some old friend of the Garioch Presbytery may read these lines, and, thinking of little links that connected him with those troublesome and stormy times, smile also, and half own that there were more Johnny Milnes in the world than one, more shadows that will remain shadows to the end.

History but repeats itself, and even with regard to the Culsalmond Psalms, we may again quote the saying *Stat nominis umbra*!

CHAPTER XXIV

LAST DAYS AT SCHOOL

"And will it breathe into him all the zeal,
That candidates for such a prize should feel,
To take the lead and be the foremost still
In all true worth and literary skill?"

Cowper.

With the close of events narrated in the last chapter, the ecclesiastical battles of the Gariocli ceased, so far at least as we were concerned, and the Latinists of Sillerton had settled down to what boys now would call a 'steady grind.'

Time was creeping on, and we were approaching that age when we were expected to push our fortune on a wider field than in the parish school. It was, indeed, no child's play that lay before us now. By 'us,' I mean half a dozen youths, not yet claiming the sweet sixteen, but closely approaching it, and grinding up, for all they were worth, the different branches of study that might land them among the list of prizemen, who by and by would reap the laurels of the annual competition at the two Aberdeen Universities, then two in everything but divinity, now happily blended into one noble institution, able and willing to educate the aspiring youth of the North. The subjects on which the competitors would be examined were simply two, namely, the rendering of English into Latin, and vice versa, or the rendering of Latin into English, or as we called it, 'version and translation.' To become proficient in these two subjects required no small amount of self-denial and study. We had a teacher fresh from academic hulls himself, and burning to send youths to the competition, who, in winning honors to themselves, would reflect a portion of that honor upon their teacher. We were then ably coached. The usual hour for school was ten, but the teacher and Latinists met at nine, so as to have a good hour of higher education, without those interruptions which were likely to occur when the ordinary scholars began the work of the day.

Every morning a version, as it was called, was given out, while the one of the day before was examined and duly rated. How anxiously we listened to the reading of the daily record! Men waiting to hear the decision of a jury that chained them or set them free, were not more anxious than we were, and when the name came with the coveted *Sine errore*, this was one of the happiest moments of our life. But, after all, was this not a foreshadowing of many a scene of after-life, where we, or such as we, must needs be judged? Are there not times when the malicious efforts of enemies may conspire to materialize a cloud around us; when treacherous lips will whisper doubtings softly to the ear, that would not dare to speak them out manfully, face to face; when appearances that in themselves meant little or nothing were so distorted and twisted by diabolical manipulation as to almost prove anything whatever, and yet, at length, when the vile attempt has broken down, when the clouds of cruel suspicion have 'rolled by,' when they who may have been led to doubt us, have found cause to give a purer and holier judgment then the verdict of our boyhood's teacher is again repeated, and to our ears comes once again the pleasing judgment *Sine errore*.

And looking beyond self, there are few who have not made some 'maxies' in the version of life. Ah! when an erring brother or maybe sister is being weighed, let, then, our gentler sympathies go forth through that indescribable feeling that links one heart to another go forth to help the weak to weigh down the beam on mercy's side. Such may be like bread cast upon the waters, that shall yet be found again, even though after many days. And when our own last account is rendered, may errors, failings, weaknesses, transgressions all be blotted out, and through the merits of One who once said nay, often said 'Though your sins be like scarlet they shall be as white as snow,' and who, though now exalted, feels as we feel, in the possession of a nature the same as ours. Then may our record, with all its imperfections, be accepted through His merits alone, and over the blurred and obliterated evidences of much shortcoming, the verdict be clearly and distinctly written *Sine errore*.

These were certainly anxious and hard times. With us, truly, there was no royal road to the grand truths contained in the writings of ancient Greece and Rome. The Latin Rudiments, from title-page to finis; Melvin's Grammar, with its hundreds of lines of Latin hexameters ; Greek grammars, Caesar, Virgil, Horace, Xenophon, and, as a species of alterative, arithmetic, algebra, and geometry thrown in this was the 'bill of fare' on which the choice youths of Sillerton were encouraged to try their mental teeth. Nor did we flinch from the ordeal. We were well coached, as stated before. The master had himself traveled over the same road. He knew every step of the way, and we never lacked encouragement to press on his motto and oars being ever 'Excelsior.' As an example of the judicious treatment we received, I shall recount an experience of my own in the earlier stages of our Latinity.

I had mastered a few hundred lines of Melvin's hexameters without any extraordinary difficulties, and to the satisfaction of the master, when suddenly a change a change for the worse came over me. My memory seemed to fail; the lines, usually so easily committed, would scarcely limp along; and lessons generally were, without doubt, a sad failure. I must have looked unhappy, but the teacher's countenance expressed despair. He quietly took me aside, asked what was the matter, and questioned me with evident anxiety if I really had lost my interest in classical studies, lost my senses, lost anything that should not have been lost. I owned up at once. Young George Washington, when he carved the paternal cherry tree without the paternal permission, was not more candid than I. I had unfortunately very unfortunately laid my hands upon one of Jane Porter's novels 'Thaddens of Warsaw' and from that ill-fated moment no line of Melvin's Grammar could find a resting-place in my memory.

I received there and then, and most kindly too, a holiday sufficiently long to enable me to finish my story; I received also at the same time some very excellent advice which I have never since forgotten. In due course the romance speedily passed away; back came the hexameters in all their beauty and smoothness; and the beam of satisfaction that played over the teacher's face as he listened to the wisdom of the old stern grammarian (known by the nickname of 'Old Grim') repeated carefully and correctly by the lips of his pupil, showed clearly that our golden age had again returned.

Summer was now among the things of the past, the golden sheaves of autumn had all been stored away in the huge cornstacks that gladdened the farmers' hearts, and adorned their courtyards. The little boys and girls of the village were looking forward anxiously to the next moon to enjoy the rustic game of 'hide and seek' among the lights and shadows that would be found there; but, alas! there was no 'hide and seek' in store for the busy Latinists.

Probably we thought and said, too, with a sigh, "Every dog has its day," and we may have had ours also among the cornstacks. 'Hide and seek' was unquestionably a fascinating game even when played by boys, but when the challenge came, 'Boys and girls come out to play,' its charms were increased a thousand-fold. It is asserted by scientists that, on even a calm ocean, there is an attraction between vessels lying near each other, that may bring them into dangerous proximity, nay, into perilous contact. And so, in the sweet game of 'hide and seek,' how often did one find himself, in the friendly shadow of the cornstacks, near some youthful maiden, whose sums he had often worked out for her, and whose hand he was, in consequence, permitted to gently press, away from the gaity and tell tale moonbeams.

Ah! much do I fear, were the truth told, that Thaddeus of Warsaw was not the only disturbing influence that crept into the parish school to cripple our hexameters; there were little episodes of romance amid even our school-days that would cross our paths to interfere at times with sterner duties, and when I think of it, the reciprocating squeeze of a gentle hand, or the kindly blink of a loving eye, did sometimes make sad havoc in our ranks. I fear, also, that in these cases we were not quite so candid as when the Polish patriot was at fault; it would have taken more than thumbscrews to make us own to the douce dominie that somebonnie Jean had come between us and our allotted tasks; we were willing to stand unlimited chaffing in such a cause; the secret, after all, was our own, and were we not acting up to the advice of our great bard, and who knew better?

> "And keep aye something
> to yoursell, ye dinna tell to ony."

The autumn games were then not for us, and when we returned to school, after our six weeks of holidays, it was only to say, 'Good-bye,' and to receive credentials to one or other of the Grammar Schools, that in Old or New Aberdeen prepared youths for the approaching competition. This course was not always adopted. Boys often remained at the parish school to the very last; but many sought the Grammar School, as affording a wider arena, where the classical athlete could find a larger number of competitors with whom to measure his own strength and prowess.

My own departure from home was accompanied with more than one trial. Leaving home with all its agreeable associations, and generally, for the first time, is far from pleasant. Looking forward to the dandy jacket of a smart 'middy,' or even to a month's fishing among the lochs and tarns of the great Grampian range, makes home-leaving anything but painful, but in our case, there was no play in prospect, but only good stern work before us; the midnight oil must needs be burned ; our lottery was not 'all prizes and no blanks;' the prizes were indeed only for a few, and when the short roll of the successful competitors should be called, at least four-fifths of the crowd would return in disappointment to their homes. Many of these last, however, would enter the classes with their more fortunate companions, but to not a few this would be denied.

Prior to the competition I ranked myself among this number. I had been given to understand that my entering the college depended entirely on my proving a successful competitor. Whether it was wise or otherwise to give such an assurance may be difficult to determine. Much might be said on both sides. Doubtless what was done was done for the best, and at all events, in the present case, while it hinted at the painful consequences of defeat, it neither weakened hand nor heart in preparing for the fray. My father, with commendable caution, had, unknown to any member of the family, procured for me the promise of a presentation bursary, in the event of my defeat at the competition, but with commendable pride he much preferred a bursary won by merit alone. Whether or not he was gratified in this, we shall see hereafter. Often have I burned the midnight oil, but never more unremittingly and faithfully than then; often have I seen the rising sun peep in at the attic window to startle eyes that had not yet tasted sleep, but there was an intenseness in the work clone then, that was never felt afterwards in the same ratio.

There was then an issue at stake that might cast sunshine or shadow over a whole lifetime an issue that, in its intensity, never seemed to be approached in after years.

My own fate seemed to lie within the compass of my own hands, and like the youthful warrior who buckled on for the first time, his maiden sword, to me victory and defeat seemed to poise upon a level beam. I knew that all Sillerton stood on tiptoe of expectation; the genial, anxious dominie never failed to send messages of encouragement and good cheer, and round the family hearth I well knew that kindly hearts felt the deepest sympathy in all my experiences, and never ceased to long and pray earnestly for a 'Godspeed.'

And thus the weeks passed by; the versions approached in correctness the models that were day by day placed before us, till *sine errore* became the rule instead of being the exception. And so also with other studies. We were approaching the end very perceptibly, and as the rector closed his book on the Saturday preceding the great day of competition, I can almost recall his parting bow before dismissing us, and hear again the fervent wish that we might distinguish ourselves in the approaching classic tournament, and shed fresh luster, not only upon ourselves, but upon the Grammar School of Old Aberdeen, nay, upon its rector as well.

Well might we have all replied, prayerfully, fervently, humbly, "So mote it be."

CHAPTER XXV

THE CONCLUSION THE COMPETITION AND THE GOWN

"He that no more must say, is listened more
Than they whom youth and ease have taught to gloze;
More are men's ends mark'd, than their lives before
The setting sun, and music at the close,
As the last taste of sweets is sweetest last;
Writ in remembrance, more than things long past."

Richard II

On a bleak morning near the end of October, between the year 1840 and a decade later, somewhat over one hundred and fifty competitors sat down in the long room of King's College, to test their skill in an academic tourney, that had, after all, but a few prizes to offer, and where also, the great majority would feel like the unhorsed knights of old, when sword and lance both lay shivered on the ground. No roll was called, for the competition was open to Scotland, or, for that matter, to the world at large; and had a 'heathen Chinee' and a fur-clad Esquimaux presented themselves at that table, they would have found a place, and, provided their Latin it was up to the mark, they had as good a chance of success as the Scottish youth who had studied his classics in some of the famous Grammar Schools of the north.

Two or three professors were on duty. Poor little Tulloch went limping round the room, as anxious and fidgety as if he were one of the competitors himself; Greek 'Habby,' though old and frail, still held his own, and looked as if, when in his prime, he would have been more likely to have proved the victor in an old-time wrestling match than to win the poet's crown at the Olympic games. And last, though not least, came burly Prosody,

165

as we always called our Professor of Humanity.

We believed, indeed, that Prosody would rather have arrayed himself in a Roman toga than encase his massive limbs in the more artificial habiliments of a modern Scot. I never looked at him without dreaming of Cicero, and it was generally believed, at least among the 'Bageants,' that Prosody thought in Latin hexameters. The version, as it was called, was slowly dictated, and thereafter we all bent ourselves resolutely to our task. The only book allowed us was the ordinary Latin dictionary, and keen eyes watched that no other tome or notes of any kind were used. The hours wore on in profound stillness, broken only by the peculiar sound that a hundred and fifty pens, operating all at the same time, make upon a hundred and fifty sheets of paper.

A change of watchmen comes, and as the guard is relieved in comes the good old Dr. Hercules Scott, with a smile upon his kindly face that told as plainly as so many words, that he personally would be glad could we all be first bursars or prizemen. Dr. Fyfe follows trippingly, and walks along with as little apparent interest as if he would gladly boil down all the Latin and mathematics in the universe in one of his own retorts. And last glides in, for all the world like a feline, the erudite Professor of Natural Philosophy. Smooth-tongued was he as 'Oily Gammon' himself, but, a stranger to our northland ways, he never gained the students hearts, and never awoke anything more than a hiss in after-days, when professors and students sought the Public Hall on occasions of discipline.

There were more professors present than those mentioned, but I have sketched, very roughly it may be, at least the principal figures. And so the day wears on. Time was called at last, and each candidate, after placing a certain number on his exercise and the same number and his name on a coupon attached, separated the two and placed the pieces in different boxes. This closed the first day's work in fact, the more important part of the competition as the translation of Latin into English was not considered by any means so drastic a test of mental capacity, as the turning of English into choice Ciceronian Latin. Next day found us at our post again, with the same guard mounted over us, and when the hours for work were exhausted time was again called, the same boxing operation took place as on the day previous, and we, alone or in small groups, wended our ways to our respective places of abode, to go over our work again in the quiet of our own rooms. to mark what errors we had made, if any, and to calculate our chances of success.

The few days that intervened between the competition days and that on which the list of prizemen or bursars would be published in the Public Hall of the College dragged very wearily along. I had examined and re-examined every word and line and sentence; idioms had all been thoroughly looked into; genders of nouns, conjugations of verbs, and rules of syntax had all been applied as a line and plummet to the double exercise, and I felt reasonably satisfied with what I had done.

The schoolmaster of Sillerton was duly communicated with and his opinion requested. His reply came We of Sillerton were pretty equally matched, so far as talents or scholarship went, but in nervous susceptibility we were indeed very different. The strain had proved too much for my comrades; they had simply lost their heads, and in consequence errors had crept in errors that might, nay, that certainly would, count heavily against them. I alone seemed likely to be successful- in my exercises there were no maxies no glaring errors; there was, in one or two places, room for improvement, but taking one thing with another, the chances of success were on my side. Mark, 'chances' only. The kindly teacher felt very confident, as he afterwards told me, but he feared to raise my hopes too high, lest

I might feel disappointment the more bitterly should I have already almost anticipated the joys of triumph.

At last the day the eventful day arrived. Accompanied by my father, who had come from Sillerton that morning with a few others equally interested, I wended my way from New to Old Aberdeen, past the canal bridge, beneath which then passed many a barge laden with the produce of the Garioch and Buchan districts; past the Red Lion of famous memory, with the Latin motto, Serva jugum, painted boldly upon its capacious signboard, and which all students, from time immemorial, persisted in translating, 'Hand round the jug' past this famous hostelry, I said, until, passing under the lofty and elegant granite crown that distinguishes the well-known and ancient seat of learning, we entered the great square, which we found crowded by hundreds, attracted thither by a motive the same as that which had drawn ourselves.

A few anxious and restless moments pass; then the old bell clangs loudly from a neighboring tower, the massive doors are thrown open, and we rush in, as if every man and boy among us firmly believed in the adage, 'Deil tak' the hindmost.' There, in a railed-in'dais, clothed in silken gowns, and wearing shiny hats, sat the members of the Senatus Academicus, prepared to disclose the secrets that were contained in a roll that lay on the bookboard before them.

Soon every sound was hushed in expectation of the approaching denouement, and I doubt not every competitor felt much as a culprit does, as the jurymen file into the room, and the foreman stands ready to make known the decision of the twelve men good and true. The sacrist, armed with the symbol of authority, approaches the dais, and laying the scepter upon the table, steps aside to await the issue of events. There is still a moment's pause, and then a whisper passes along the professorial line, and seems particularly directed to the center figure of the group.

I at once recognize a very aged man, whom I had observed while we were waiting outside, approaching the great hall door, leaning on the arm of a lady, who there left him in the care of one of the College officials. This I learned afterwards to be Principal Jack, now, of course, relieved from duty, except, perhaps, when his venerable appearance and great age would tend to add additional dignity to a professorial meeting. I observed also at a glance that the old Principal was blind.

As he rose slowly to his feet, the other members of the Senatus rose; the roll of names was placed in the old man's hands, and the Professor standing next to him seemed ready to whisper each name, as it came in order of merit, to the Principal's ear. I need not say how awful was the silence now. At last, at last it was broken; the whispered name came in measured, yet in tremulous tones from the old Principal's lips, and one shout of triumph rose 'loud and long' from the friends and relatives of the successful first bursar, who now stepped forward at the beck of the sacrist to a place of honor nearer the Professorial line.

Another and another name is called, and my hopes are beginning to sink low. Ten or eleven names have been called, and yet Sillerton is unrepresented among the beaming line of happy faces now lifted immeasurably above all the rest. The twelfth name comes. Can it be possible? Can I be deceived? Could there be another of the same name? No major, no minor is appended. A hearty shout greets my victory; a dozen friendly hands push me forward, and Donald Andrew, of Sillerton, stands among the acclaimed bursars of King's College and University of Aberdeen. Little more remains to be told. The same afternoon my delighted father had me arrayed in cap and gown in one of the famous clothing establishments of Bon-Accord.

I would have fain taken a run to Sillerton to spend a quiet day at home, and in truth I needed it, and perhaps to enjoy the congratulations of my friends and acquaintances there, but this might not be. There was no railroad in those days to Sillerton, and matriculation day was close at hand. I decided to remain, and that evening I saw my father off on the old 'Defiance' mail-coach. "Good-bye, Donald, and God bless you," said the old man, cheerily, in a dialect learned in school on the banks of the Spey, learned as Sillerton boys learned their Latin and Greek, and which still, on occasions, even after the lapse of so many years, I sometimes seem to hear as the softened echo of a familiar voice gently thrown back from a distant hill. "Wherever you are," he said, "never forget that you are a gentleman."

As the driver gathered together the reins in his hand, and the scarlet-coated guard gave the last signal on his official horn that Her Majesty's 'Defiance' was ready to start on its journey northward, he had only time to add, "I will remember you kindly to the schoolmaster, and to your other friends in Sillerton, nor will I forget to tell all at home that you looked right well in your King's College Cap and Grown."

THE END

Made in the USA
Monee, IL
13 December 2020

52915969R00095